RICK & BUBBA

FOR PRESIDENT

The Two Sexiest Fat Men Alive
Take on Washington

RICK & BUBBA
FOR PRESIDENT

The Two Sexiest Fat Men Alive
Take on Washington

By

**Rick Burgess
and
Bill "Bubba" Bussey**

with Martha Bolton

THOMAS NELSON
Since 1798

NASHVILLE   DALLAS   MEXICO CITY   RIO DE JANEIRO   BEIJING

Published in Nashville, Tennessee, by Thomas Nelson. Thomas Nelson is a registered trademark of Thomas Nelson, Inc.

Published in association with the literary agency of Sanford Communications, Inc., Portland, Oregon.

Thomas Nelson, Inc. titles may be purchased in bulk for educational, business, fund-raising, or sales promotional use. For information, please e-mail SpecialMarkets@ThomasNelson.com.

Scripture references, unless otherwise marked, are taken from The Holy Bible, The New King James Version®. © 1982 by Thomas Nelson, Inc. Used by permission. All rights reserved.

Library of Congress Cataloging-in-Publication Data

Burgess, Rick.
    Rick and Bubba for president : the two sexiest fat men take on Washington / by Rick Burgess and Bill "Bubba" Bussey.
      p. cm.
    ISBN 978-0-8499-1878-0
    1. Presidents—United States—Election—Humor. 2. United States—Politics and government—Humor. I. Bussey, Bubba. II. Title.
PN6231.P693B84 2008
818'.602—dc22   2007052524

Printed in the United States of America

08 09 10 11 12 RRD 9 8 7 6 5 4 3 2 1

We dedicate this book to our military men and women
who are serving this country and protecting freedom
around the world. You are a different breed of human being,
and for your sacrifice we can never thank you enough.

CONTENTS

CONTENTS

CONTENTS

CONTENTS

ACKNOWLEDGMENTS

First and foremost, we thank our Savior Jesus Christ. You came not to take life, but to give us life, that we may have it abundantly. We thank you for loving us enough to die in our place and defeat sin and death once and for all. Thank you for offering the only real peace that can only be obtained through GOD'S grace through you, His Son (see John 16:33).

We would also like to thank:

Our wives, Sherri and Betty. You are living proof that a man who has a godly wife has a good thing.

Our children—you are all a true blessing from God.

Rick: Brandi, Blake, Brooks, and Brody. (AKA: Jo Jo, Boomer, Big Love, and Taz—The Killer Bs)

Bubba: Hunter and Katelyn

And in loving memory of Bonner "Cornbread" Burgess. God has used your short two-and-a-half years on this earth to impact lives around the world. We look forward to being with you in eternity. In the meantime, we will be about our Father's business and continue to see the impact of your life for the rest of our days on earth.

Our parents for raising us to know better (even though we don't always accomplish this).

The entire Rick and Bubba staff (thirteen years together and still going):

Calvin "Speedy" Wilburn, Don Juan DeMarco Williams, Ryan Greenwood, Scott "The Tech Guy" Ferguson, Jim Dunaway, Ken "Bones" Hearns, James Spann, Mark Gentle, and interns past, present, and future.

Thank you to our parent company, Cox Broadcasting, to the staff at Thomas Nelson, to David Sanford, David Marsh, and Bob Carey and everyone at Syndicated Solutions.

Special thanks to Martha Bolton. (You're probably sick of Rick and Bubba by now.)

Note from Martha: Are you kidding? Never!

Super special thanks to our radio affiliates across the country and everyone who listens to our program. Without you, we would just be two fat guys talking to each other.

INTRODUCTION
WHY? WHY NOT?

Why are two radio personalities from Alabama running for the co-presidency of the United States? Aren't there already enough contenders in the presidential race? Even a comedian and threw his hat into the ring! (Like many of you, we had a hard time figuring out which one that was, too.)

For the record—and so there is no problem with the Election Board—we are not seeking to have our names printed on the ballot. We understand that talk show host and funnyman Stephen Colbert actually took out election papers to declare his candidacy in at least one state. That costs money; therefore, we will not be doing that. Instead, we are going after the "write-in vote." If enough people want us to run (and they remember how to spell our names), we are willing to go to Washington and lead our country for the next four or eight years. If they don't, we are willing to go to Disney World and forget the whole thing. We're easy.

We also care deeply about our country. We think the direction America is heading (no trans fats, no white bread, and no sugar) is a dangerous one. Are we all blind? Don't we see what's happening? This is a ploy by our enemies to make us weak. They are trying to get us so hungry for carbs that we'll surrender everything at the first offer of a good cheeseburger.

So, to introduce our platform, the first thing we will do if we are elected co-presidents is to bring sanity back to the American diet. We grew up on white bread. We ate enough trans fats to plug up Niagara Falls. Sugar was one of our food groups. And we're both still here.

We think the leading candidates and talking heads are missing one important distinction in the political debate: America is known as the land of the free. But our forefathers never meant for it to be *calorie*-free. Where is that in the Constitution?

We want America to finally get the worldwide respect and honor she deserves. We believe we can help make some positive changes in our country. We want to do whatever we can to be a part of the solution, instead of part of the problem. But the main reason we're running for office is to get our citizens off of this whole dieting kick.

And of course, there are all those campaign dinners, too.

So read on to find out where we stand on the issues, what changes we would propose, and what life would be like under a Rick and Bubba co-presidency. Hopefully, you'll be enlightened, have some laughs, and realize what a great country our nation is—with or without the two sexiest fat men alive in office.

ADVANTAGES OF CO-PRESIDENTS

The idea of a co-presidency is relatively new to the American political scene. The closest we've come to such a concept is Bill and Hillary Clinton, or Hillary and Bill, depending on the election year.

The idea has some merit, and some say it's long overdue. That is why this November you will have the opportunity to elect a new type of candidate. We want to be the first official co-presidency candidates in America.

What are the advantages of a Rick and Bubba co-presidency?

★ We could save the country a fortune by taking advantage of two-for-one specials at all the Washington DC eating spots.

★ When one of us makes a mistake, we could blame it on the other one and leave the usual scapegoat, the vice-president, completely out of it.

★ At press conferences we could interview each other and not leave anything to unpredictable reporters.

★ The way our system works now, very few Americans ever get the opportunity to serve as president. If we start electing dual presidents, or someday maybe even group presidents, it will substantially increase all of our chances of one day getting to live in the White House.

★ Americans will be able to take comfort knowing their president is well rested: When we go on *Meet the Press* one of us can take a nap while the other one answers the questions.

★ If one of us chokes on a pretzel, the other one will be nearby to do the Heimlich.

★ Sometimes it takes more than one president to keep Congress in line.

★ If one of us loses our place in the State of the Union address, the other one can take over for him.

★ If one of us gets the nuclear codes mixed up with, say, our checking account number, the other one will probably catch the mistake.

★ And finally, the idea of a Rick and Bubba co-presidency is such a novel idea, we get to write a novel about it. (Okay, so it's nonfiction, but authors are always mixing up those concepts nowadays anyway.)

OUR CAMPAIGN STRATEGY

Every political campaign needs a plan of action. You have to know how you're going to take the northern states, the eastern states, the West, and of course, the South. And most importantly, you have to know which states typically have the best food at their rallies.

We don't mean to be presumptuous, but we believe that we could carry the Southern vote hands down. Southerners have a history of preferring one of their own in the White House. It's sort of like having a relative living there; you can plan a stopover on your next RV trip and save on motel expenses.

Southerners are very patriotic, too. We stand for God, country, and apple pie. The two of us are so patriotic that at times we'll even have seconds on the apple pie. If it's the Fourth of July, we may eat the whole thing.

Another reason we're confident we'll be able to carry the South is that we both have plenty of relatives living there. We could take the whole state of Alabama if just our families showed up at the polls.

The western region of our country is a little more difficult to carry, mainly due to the fact that it has California. Californians use hummus as a dip. We're not saying it's unpatriotic to do this. We're just saying that a bowl of squashed garbanzo beans is not a dip. Salsa is a dip. Cheese is a dip. Hummus is a caulking substance. This discrepancy could be a source of contention between us and the Golden State. Californians want someone in the White House who is on the same page when it comes to health food. We're not on the same page. We're not even in the same book. We won't eat tofu, bean sprouts, or liver pâté. Not even for votes. We have our principles.

We're not going to totally write off California, however. After all, they did give us Ronald Reagan, one of the greatest presidents America has ever known. (We don't think he ate hummus either.)

We might do all right in the Northeast, even with New York. New Yorkers tend to vote Democratic, but they also like to eat. In this instance, our eating habits might work in our favor. New Yorkers pride themselves in being inclusive and politically correct. When you think about it, isn't health food all about discrimination? When we sponsor public service announcements about Americans and their unhealthy diets, aren't we discriminating against those citizens who happen to like calories?

We think so. That is why part of our platform will be to bring this nation back to a nondiscriminatory diet. We welcome eaters of all shapes and sizes, tastes, and preferences to join our campaign. We will not discriminate against white bread consumers. How narrow-minded and bigoted is that? We will not give special privileges to whole-grain eaters just because they can eat the roughage equivalent of a small patio for lunch. New Yorkers will appreciate our open-minded stance on this, which could actually give us a win in the Northeast.

Our handlers have assured us that the Midwest should also be ours for the taking. (We don't really have handlers. It just sounds more official. The only handlers we have are our wives.) Since the Midwest has Chicago, another city that likes to eat, we figure the calorie-discrimination issue should play well there, too. We also believe that hummus is actually outlawed in Chicago, so that should go a long way in helping us take the Midwestern vote.

Granted, we might have a little trouble with the Northwest. Some of the voters and politicians in Washington and Oregon have gotten a few funny ideas over the years. Like euthanasia. Remember the euthanasia controversy some years back? Washington and Oregon were the two states that wanted such a law. Our platform is adamantly opposed to euthanasia, so we might lose a few votes in the Northwest. But we don't care. When we get old and sick, we don't want someone coming along and pulling the plug on us before our time. If they trip over it and it's an honest mistake, that's one thing. But other than that, we want to go out naturally. In fact, we're kind of looking forward to lingering. It sounds kind of quiet and peaceful. You get to be with your family and pass the day away without a lot of interference from the outside world. The medical staff doesn't go poking around on you with sharp objects either because they figure it's just a matter of time before your bed becomes available.

When a month turns into two, and two months turn into two years or even longer, the deathwatch visits start to die off and everyone returns to life as normal. Meanwhile, you just keep right on lingering. You might even surprise everyone by still being around ten or twenty years past your presumed date of expiration, like some of the stuff in our refrigerators. This sort of thing has been known to happen. That's why we don't want anyone writing us off until God says it's time for us to go home.

If we don't take the Northwest because of our stand on euthanasia (actually, we believe most northwestern voters have changed their minds on this subject and have since voted against it), then we still have the rest of the country to help us win enough votes to sweep the Electoral College.

Yes, the foundation of our election system all comes down to electoral votes, doesn't it? But what does anybody really know about the Electoral College, anyway? It has never made a lot of sense to us. How is it that you can win the popular vote, but still lose in the Electoral College? If the majority of the people vote for you, shouldn't that make you the winner?

Apparently, this is the problem: If America did not have the Electoral College, then that would mean that the states with the highest population, such as California and New York, would always determine who runs the country for all the rest of the states. The Electoral College spreads the power around a little more evenly. This way, the heartland voters can be heard almost as loudly as the voters on both coasts.

So the rules are that you have to win the country on a state-by-state basis. That's why Rhode Island counts for something. And that's why on election night you'll hear the newscasters keeping track of how many states have gone red and how many states have gone blue. Over the years it has changed as to which party is which color. But even so, when the whole map of the United States is nearly all blue or all red, it means a landslide victory for that candidate, as it was with Ronald Reagan. Much of the time, the states will be more evenly divided, and a candidate will only win by a handful of Electoral College votes.

If, on Election Day, it starts looking like the Rick and Bubba ticket is going to need to carry California in order to win the election, then, and only then, will we be open to accepting some California hummus.

Our bathroom tiles could probably use it anyway.

FOREIGN AFFAIRS

One question that will be on the minds of all voters when they go to the polls this November is this: Who is the best man or woman to lead our nation when it comes to foreign affairs?

The answer is simple: We are.

The presidential team of Rick and Bubba will make America strong again. We won't let foreign countries push us around. And we will personally travel to every other nation to eat with their leaders. Yes, we said *eat*. That's how committed we are to our country.

Ronald Reagan once said, "All great change in America happens at the dinner table." We would like to carry this idea further and say, "All great change in the *world* happens at the dinner table." Imagine how much better we would all get along if we'd just eat together a little more often. We're not talking all those fancy state dinners either. We're talking barbeques, meat and threes, chili feeds, ice cream socials, and potlucks on the White House lawn.

Another thing that we would change in the foreign affairs department is how we deal with rogue nations. The problem with Iran's Mahmoud Ahmadinejad and North Korea's Kim Jong Il is that we're trying to make them answer to United Nations mandates. Everyone knows that the United Nations doesn't have a lot of muscle when it comes to enforcing its mandates; it's more about slapping fines here and there, and threatening with menacing terms like "embargos" and "trade restrictions." (We're trembling in our boots, aren't you?)

We have come up with an innovative plan to keep these defiant leaders in line: an International Homeowners Association. That's right, a world-wide HOA could be the perfect entity to handle these problems. Homeowners Association boards take no prisoners. No country would dare defy the order of an HOA. HOAs put teeth into their threats, and they leave nothing to debate.

If the United Nations operated more like the typical HOA board, there is no way that rogue leaders would dare to defy them. We're sure that neither Mahmoud nor Kim could handle the steady stream of letters, warnings, citations, and nasty phone calls that an HOA board is capable of setting into motion.

In fact, if President Bush had sent an HOA board over to Iraq to deal with Saddam Hussein in the first place, *they* would have found those weapons of mass destruction. Even if there truly weren't any there, they still would have found them. That's how good some HOA boards can be. They would have even found Osama bin Laden by now, especially if he was behind on his association dues.

That's what gets so frustrating to us. America has the means to take care of all the bullies of the world; we're just not utilizing our own resources. Now for you sensitive citizens out there, let us clarify that not all HOA boards bully their homeowners, but there are more than enough qualified bully board members in our nation to take care of all our foreign affairs problems.

Still not convinced? We ask you who was it that made some of our nation's subdivisions take down their American flags commemorating 9/11? Was it terrorists? Communist spies? No. It was HOA boards, that's who! And what happened? Most of the people they confronted eventually folded and complied with their order. That's how afraid we are of them.

America can have its Navy Seals. We can have our Green Berets and our Special Forces. We can have the toughest Secretary of State in the history of our nation. But all of them put together won't hold a candle to the power of an HOA board.

We'll prove it to you.

LETTER FROM HOA BOARD

RE: Illegal Wall in East Berlin
Dear Neighbor and Leader of East Germany:

It has come to our attention that you have constructed a wall that does not meet with the regulations listed in your CC and Rs. This is in direct violation of the agreement which you signed. Consider this your first warning. If you do not tear down the illegal wall immediately, our board will have no choice but to come onto your property and remove it ourselves. Don't think we'll do it? Try us. Your puny weaponry is no match for our determination to win this battle. You may think you can bully the rest of the world, but you will not push us around. According to Section 4036 of our HOA rules, no wall shall be erected over five feet in height, nor that does not enhance the beauty of the neighborhood. Your wall fails on both accounts. Frankly, it is ugly. We expect your wall to be down before our HOA inspector drives by the property again next Thursday. There will be dire consequences for noncompliance. We suggest you cooperate. Thank you for your prompt attention to this matter.

Sincerely,
Your HOA Board

LETTER FROM HOA BOARD

RE: Illegal Nuke Testing
Dear Mr. Kim Jong Il:

Some of your neighbors have complained about your unapproved missile launchings from your rear yard in the middle of the night. It is their concern that you are testing nukes, which, as you know, is against HOA rules. We are going to have to ask you to cease this practice immediately. If you do not comply with this request, your clubhouse privileges will be suspended, your fines doubled, your firstborn possibly held for ransom, and we will be forced to give you a manicure the hard way, if you know what we mean. We do not wish to cause unnecessary friction with your country. However, it is fully our intention to maintain a certain standard of living for our entire world community. Your nuke testing interferes with the tone we would like to set, and we simply cannot tolerate it any longer.

Sir, we trust that you will comply with this action and prevent us from taking more drastic measures. We have a few secret weapons of our own that we are not afraid to use if you choose to disregard this notice.

Sincerely,
Your HOA board

LETTER FROM HOA BOARD

RE: Your disappearance and overdue status on account
Dear Mr. Bin Laden:

You can run, Mr. Bin Laden, but you cannot hide from us. We happen to know that you are currently ten years in arrears on your HOA dues. Rest assured, we will track you down, sir. It does not matter in what cave in what country you happen to be hiding at the moment. Our entire board is hot on your trail, and we will bring you current on your account if it is the last thing we do. We realize there are others who would like to get their hands on you, too, namely our president. But hear us on this, sir. We will find you first. And if there is anything left of you by the time we're through, then our government authorities can have you. You have ignored our past-due letters for the last time, Mr. Bin Laden. We are going to collect if we have to sell your beard on eBay to do it!

Have a nice day,
Your HOA Board

Perhaps you never thought of HOA boards as a secret weapon and potential insurance for world peace, but we have, and it's ideas like this that qualify us for the highest position in the land.

THE NATIONAL DEBT

As candidates for co-presidents of the United States, we assure you that we are both committed to getting rid of the national debt once and for all. Following is our threefold plan:

First a clarification: don't a lot of people around the world owe us money? It seems to us they do. If we remember correctly, didn't Kuwait promise to pay us a good chunk of change if we helped them get Saddam Hussein out of their country? Did we do our part? Yes. Did they do theirs? As far as we know, the check is still in the mail.

We believe it's high time that America started collecting some of these outstanding debts. If we have to, we can get a collection agency involved. Let some debt collector call these leaders at the same time every night for a few weeks, preferably during dinner, until they can get them to agree to some sort of payment arrangement.

How much longer are we going to keep extending these notes? If we need money, and apparently we could use about a trillion dollars or so, it just makes economic sense to call in a few of these overdue accounts, doesn't it? Wouldn't that be what any of us would do with our own personal finances? I mean, if someone borrowed a thousand dollars from you, say, fifty or sixty years ago, and they still haven't paid it off, wouldn't you think it's time you brought it up over coffee?

Then, there are all the late fees. What about them? If a country is late with its payments to us, couldn't we use the opportunity to hike up their interest rate to about thirty percent and charge them a significant late fee, which would then push them over their limit so we could tack on an over-limit fee, too? When they finally do make a payment, we could then charge a 3 percent transaction fee on top of that. If this type of bill collecting is working for MasterCard and VISA, shouldn't it work for the good ol' USA?

If you've been reading the papers, or perhaps even your mail, you know that collecting debt has become a very profitable business these days. Think about it—when's the last time you saw a major credit card company or a bank working out of a trailer? They have thirty- and forty-story office buildings and appear to be doing very well. America could learn a lot from these businesses on how to manage debt collection.

While we're at it, why don't we ask all the people of the world who are free today because of America's help to drop a donation in the mail and earmark it for paying off our national debt? Sort of like passing an international collection plate. We don't think that's asking too much, do you? It would simply be a "You were there for us, America, so we want to be there for you now" kind of goodwill gesture. We think a little show of international gratitude is long overdue, about as overdue as all of their payments.

Another plan we have to raise money for our national debt is to turn the White House into a bed and breakfast. Now hear us out on this. The White House has that Southern plantation kind of look that is so popular with the bed and breakfast crowd. It also has one hundred and thirty-two different rooms. And besides, Bill Clinton used it in a similar manner during his stay at the White House, except he didn't charge. Think of all the revenue he missed!

We figure we could charge between two to three hundred dollars per night per room (you've probably spent that at Disney World, maybe not for the room, but for everything your kids ate from the room refrigerator). In the off-season, we would cut the price of a White House room down to about eighty bucks. That way, it'll be affordable for the majority of Americans. Imagine your wife asking where you're taking her for your next anniversary, and you'll be able to say, "We're going to the Inn at 1600 Pennsylvania Avenue!" How cool would that be?

Of course, we can't do this during times of war, or when our national security risk is at a high level. But during those periods of relative calm, a White House bed and breakfast could bring in a lot of much-needed extra cash.

We might even include an Oval Office photo op in the package for an extra hundred dollars or so. (Of course, if we're the presidents, you'd get two for the price of one.)

Another way to get rid of the national debt would be to cut back on some of these government grants that we've been throwing around lately. One study funded by our government researched the mating habits of the monarch butterfly. That study resulted in the shocking observation that the female monarch is attracted to the male monarch.

We believe that was called the "Duh Study."

A different grant was for a study that ended up proving that men and women are different. We don't know if you are as blown away by this discovery as we were, but news like this has the potential of completely changing life as we know it. Men and women could start demanding separate restroom facilities, their own clothing sections in department stores, their own special-interest magazines, their own medical specialists . . . where will it all end?

Wait a minute, they already have their own restrooms, their own clothing sections, their own magazines, and their own specialists. *Why didn't someone tell us that before we spent all that money to find out?!*

Under a Rick and Bubba co-presidency, these kinds of wasteful government grants will be a thing of the past. Every grant application will have to be personally approved by us. Naturally, we would fund all the good research projects, like trying to find a cure for cancer, AIDS, and other national health concerns. But if the research is merely to find out something that we or anyone with a preschool education already knows, then the grant will be denied. There's no more discussion on the matter. If monarch butterflies need more information other than instinct during mating season, that's their problem.

We would also raise money by targeting the cults. By that, we mean all the Star Wars fans, Trekkies, Lord of the Ring fans—all those people who camp out the night before the next movie release—and we would actively enlist their help. We could hold conventions in several cities throughout America, and then add, say, a five-dollar surcharge to the price of each admission ticket (apparently, there is no limit to what these fans are willing to pay to get into these conventions). Once collected, we would have them send the extra money to Washington. By our calculations, our nation could be completely out of debt in about three years.

This concept might also work with concert tickets. We could add twenty dollars to Barbra Streisand tickets (or better yet, Hannah Montana), and likewise, have the venue operators send the extra money to Washington. It would probably make Barbra feel better knowing that, if Congress doesn't raise our taxes, at least she'll be helping pay off the national debt in this very special way.

This brings us to another point that we should bring up here. Do you know that there is absolutely nothing in our tax law that prohibits ordinary citizens from sending the government more money than they need to each year when they file their income taxes? If their tax is only $10,000, but they want to write a check to the government for $100,000, they have every right to do that. No one will stop them, least of all Uncle Sam. They can give whatever amount they want and feel as good as they want about it. That's one of the freedoms of our great country. If Ted Turner wants to write a check to Uncle Sam just like he wrote one to the United Nations, he is absolutely free to do that.

Unfortunately, a lot of people don't know this. That's why, if elected, we plan to implement the Rick and Bubba "Put Your Money Where Your Mouth Is" campaign. If anyone rants and raves about some program that our government isn't providing to whatever group of people they think need it, we are going to allow them to step up to the plate, put their money where their mouth is, and pay for it themselves. That way, it's a win-win for all of us. The program gets funded, the government doesn't go into any more debt, and we don't have to hear them griping anymore.

You may think we're making light of these financial issues, but believe us, America's debt problem has become quite serious. We don't need any more debt. Once you hit the negative trillion-dollar mark in your checkbook, you've really got to start looking into your spending habits.

That is why, if elected, we pledge to put Congress on Dave Ramsey's envelope plan. Every week, we would give each member of Congress an envelope of money to spend. Once that's gone, they would have to wait until the following week to get more money to spend.

If a major bill was coming up for which they needed financing, they would have to save up their envelopes until they had enough to pay for it. This system works in America's homes; it should work for Congress, too.

Another way for us to lower our debt is to cut down on the business lunches of Congress. Let's face it; do any of them look all that hungry to you? Why should the taxpayer be footing the bill for all of these lunches and dinners? Cutting down on Ted Kennedy's lunch tab alone would probably put us in the black.

Don't think we're picking on Ted. We mentioned him because, like us, he obviously enjoys a good meal. That common bond might help bridge our and Ted's political differences once we reach office. And be assured, we don't want the taxpayers footing our lunch tab, either. A bill like that could easily triple the national debt and throw us into the greatest recession of our nation's history.

CAMPAIGN FUNDS

To run a successful presidential campaign, you need money. Apparently, lots of money. We don't have lots of money. Like we've already said, we're content with the blessings that God has given us.

The reality is, though, if you're going to run for political office, you have to raise funds for your campaign. We think we have come up with the perfect way to raise all the money we need.

We are going to our fan base for donations. Now before you start thinking that we have turned into typical politicians who are just after your wallets, hear us out. (We are after your wallets, but first we're going to show you how painless this is going to be.)

A long time ago, back when we were first doing our radio show, we had a dream. It wasn't as noble as Martin Luther King's dream. Or probably even your dreams. But it was our dream: We wanted our very own giant T-shirt-shooting hot dog. (In case you weren't with us then, we mean a larger-than-life hot dog that would hurl T-shirts emblazoned with our faces into the arms of screaming fans.)

Okay, maybe it was your dream, too.

This giant hot dog was something that was going to catapult, no pun intended, our careers into superstardom. We would use it at all our remote events. We would stand on stage and shoot Rick and Bubba T-shirts out into the cheering crowd. We realize we could have just handed out the T-shirts instead, but the giant hot dog seemed to add a bit of flair. *We had to have it!*

There was only one problem: it was expensive and we didn't have the money for it. Realizing that our growing base of Rick and Bubba supporters might be willing to help us out, we took our need to the airwaves. We announced that this was our dream and told everyone how they could help us achieve it.

Now, you've got to get this mental picture. This was back when our main radio advertisement was Bubba's Jeep Cherokee on which we had written the words, "Listen to Rick and Bubba," along with the show's radio frequency, in black shoe polish. (Talk about hard times; John Edwards has nothing on us.) We later used my (Rick) Astro Van that didn't have a working reverse gear. It was yellow, and we completely covered it in Rick and Bubba logos. Are you getting the idea of our desperate situation? (Our speechwriter's working on tweaking the story for heart-wrenching emotion so we can use it on the campaign.)

We started asking our listeners if they would help us buy the T-shirt-shooting giant hot dog by sending in money to the station. To our amazement, they did. It wasn't before long before a giant T-shirt-shooting hot dog was part of the Rick and Bubba organization. And it was all to the credit of our loyal fans.

We figure we could do the same thing with our presidential run. We'll go to our fan base and ask for their financial support. We realize the co-presidency of the United States isn't the same as a giant T-shirt-shooting hot dog, but we believe in their hearts that our fans will understand our need and once again come to our aid.

And if they don't send in enough money to fund our campaign, maybe it will be at least enough to get a new T-shirt-shooting replica of the Statue of Liberty for our rallies. Let's see our opponents top that!

NEWBIES

One of the advantages of a Rick and Bubba co-presidency is that neither one of us has ever been in politics before. Not knowing what we're doing should work to our advantage, just as it has done in all our previous jobs.

Being newcomers to the political scene also means that we have not yet been corrupted by the electoral process. We don't owe anyone any favors, nor do we have any axes to grind. We're not saying that any of the other candidates would take the oath of office and then start paying back his or her friends with government positions, or punishing their enemies with tax audits. But the temptation is there. We want you to know up front that we are above that kind of nepotism or vengeful behavior. No freebie government payroll positions from us (except for immediate family members and longtime loyal coworkers and employees, of course, and—oh yeah—that nice server at Ben and Jerry's), and only our nastiest enemies would get a visit from the tax man.

Besides being new to the political scene, we also have that carefree "Hey, we don't need the money" factor. Ross Perot had it, too. Remember Ross? He didn't need the money because he already had plenty of it. What was another four hundred thousand dollars a year or so in salary going to do for him? To Ross, it was petty cash. If he got to serve as president, he would be doing it out of sheer commitment to our country—plus the fact that he still had more charts and graphs to show on the evening news.

Mitt Romney has made this same pledge, about the money, that is. He said that if elected, he would probably forfeit the presidential salary, just as he forfeited his governor's salary. Why? Because he doesn't need the money either.

Like both of these men, we, too, don't need the money. Not because we have an abundance of cash. We don't. We just don't *need* a lot more. Like the apostle Paul in the Bible, we have learned to be content in whatever state we're in. If we're broke, we're content. If we're rich, we're content. If we're hungry . . . well, none of us is perfect.

Do you have any idea how freeing it is to not need money? If you don't *need* your job, then you could walk in and ask for a raise every other day, without worrying about getting fired. Wouldn't that be a fun way to work? No more grumbling about your crummy working conditions and how unappreciated you are. You could get it all off your chest. Then, if you choose to stay, and they want you, you could. Or if you want to look around for something else to do, you could do that, too. The whole money thing wouldn't be a factor.

If we win the presidency, we want to be happy. We don't want to feel like we owe anyone anything. We owe enough people already. Why would we want to owe the whole country? We just want to get up, walk downstairs to the Oval Office, and go about our business. When we think we've put in a good day's work, we want to be able to turn on the television set and watch a ballgame. If they impeach us over that, it wouldn't devastate us because, once again, we don't need the money.

Now, don't misunderstand. Just because we don't need the presidential income doesn't mean we won't cash the check. We wouldn't want to offend our forefathers who put this idea into practice. If they felt the president should have a salary, and if Congress has voted on its increase over the years, who are we to look down our noses on such a gift?

The only point we're making is that we are content with our lifestyle at the level it is right now. The White House is nice, but our real homes suit us just fine. They're not mansions, but they're more than comfortable. We have enough money to eat, keep a roof over our heads, put gas in our cars (most of the time), and to send our kids to school with an adequate lunch. When our term in Washington is up, we will be perfectly happy to go back to Alabama. We won't look around for another government position so we can stay in Washington on the nation's payroll. We'll serve out our term, and then happily pack up and head on out. And don't worry. We won't be taking any of the White House furniture with us as souvenirs either. We've got enough stuff already. Besides, it'd raise too many questions at the garage sale.

THE RICK AND BUBBA
PRESIDENTIAL LIBRARY

We like to think ahead. Once we win the election, life for us is likely to get so busy that we won't have time to think, much less plan our presidential library. So we thought we would get a head start and plan ours now.

First of all, we are not into this practice of treating our former presidents like royalty. They certainly should be honored, but we don't ever remember addressing them as "King" George, Bill, Ronald, or Ike. We don't have royalty here in America. Some politicians are not aware of this. But it is a fact. America does not have a king (unless you count that fast food burger guy, but he's a little creepy). We have never had a queen, either (Leona Helmsley just acted like one). We don't have a royal family (Sorry, Kennedys). We have *elected servants* who are supposed to serve their country for a period of time before returning to their homes.

Our presidential library will not be a shrine. It will be warm and inviting, with a reasonable entrance fee. Again, we don't need the money, but out of respect for our public, we won't refuse it.

The main reception area of our library will be like walking into a hunting lodge. We want oversized comfortable chairs and plenty of high fat-content snacks around. There will be lots of wildlife mounted on the walls, and maybe a few congressmen and certain reporters (depending on how our term went).

In our theater room we will show a short film outlining the real history of our presidency, not one that only shows the parts we like. We understand how former presidents can fall into the trap of editing out the bad parts of a presidency, but we want to show it all—decisions that worked, decisions that backfired, and whatever irreplaceable heirlooms our kids might have broken during our stay in the White House.

The books on display in our library will be easy to read. Not one book without pictures will be featured. The only exception will be our own books, which will all be lined up on one shelf, including several copies of this one.

While we're on the subject of books, can we vent a little here? Why is it that everyone tells the American public that instead of watching so much television or listening to the radio, they should be reading books? Then publishers go and put books on tape.

Does anyone else see the irony in this? A book on tape . . . isn't that basically radio? Not that we're against books on tape. In fact, we're still waiting for our books to be put on tape, voiced by James Earl Jones. But you do see our point, don't you?

Women who visit our library will find plenty to do. We'll have a ladies section, designed by our wives, that will cater to the interests of women. The purpose of this section, of course, is to keep the ladies occupied so that their husbands can go to the husband room where sporting events will be openly discussed. Any sports-loving female wishing to join us may do so. We won't discriminate, but a basic understanding of the game of football is required for admittance.

We've researched many other presidential libraries around the country and, to be perfectly honest, they all seem a little solemn and formal. There aren't a lot of laughs to be had in any of them, at least not as many as some of these men gave us during their administrations. For some reason, when a president leaves Washington, he suddenly wants to turn "presidential" on us. Never mind how he may have acted in office. When it comes to his library he wants us to forget his mistakes and let history record his presidential successes. But good comedy doesn't come from things that go right. It comes from things that go wrong. So what if some of a president's decisions weren't the best and everyone gave him a hard time? He's out now. He should have a little fun with it all.

That's why we're committed to making our presidential library fun. We might even have an amusement park on the property. If some of our former presidents had thought of this, their libraries would probably double in attendance. Think about it, Ronald Reagan's Library could have the Trickle Down Economics Log Ride, Jimmy Carter's could have the Economy Roller Coaster (what better way to remember the double digit inflation and double digit unemployment under the Carter years?), and the Richard Nixon Library could have the Watergate Water Show, a spectacular dancing waters show programmed to a recording of the William Tell Overture. Then, right in the middle of it, there will be eighteen and a half minutes of silence.

Even though we've already ordered our blueprints, we've decided to hold up construction on our presidential library until after the election. It just seems like better timing that way.

But we are going ahead and collecting all the picture books we can find, just in case.

RICK AND BUBBA "LIVE FROM THE WHITE HOUSE"

The concept of a weekly presidential radio address is nothing new. Many of our presidents have done one, including Ronald Reagan, George W. Bush, and Bill Clinton, to name a few.

Being radio personalities already, not only would we continue this tradition, but our weekly radio address could actually be a strong point of our co-presidency. One thing's for sure, we would work hard at making our radio address less boring than some of our predecessors. Our format would include many of the radio events that we do now on our morning radio show.

For instance, we would still do our annual Frozen Turkey Toss every November, only it would be held on the front lawn of the White House. For those of you who may not get the Rick and Bubba radio broadcast in your area and so are unfamiliar with the Frozen Turkey Toss, let us explain: The Frozen Turkey Toss is basically lawn bowling with frozen turkeys, and it is a very popular event in Birmingham every year. (Not a lot happens in Birmingham.) Since we have elected a few turkeys to office, it seems to us that Washington DC, would be a perfect place to continue the annual Frozen Turkey Toss.

As for the tradition of one turkey receiving a presidential pardon every Thanksgiving and being granted its freedom, let us assure you that under our administration, it is not gonna happen. There will be no turkey reprieves while we are in office. We will wait until they bring out the chosen turkey, and then, just as the crowd is gazing into its poor pleading eyes, we will say, "Sorry, Tom, not this year! *Off with his head!*"

That may seem heartless to some of you, but we've thought the matter through carefully. It's Thanksgiving and he's a turkey. (That pretty much sums up our reasoning.) Despite the surprised look on ol' Tom's face, we will not waver on this issue. We realize this will probably cost us the turkey vote, but we can deal with it.

Another radio bit that we might have fun doing from the White House is the *Good Ol' Boy Theater*. This is where I (Bubba) read Shakespeare. *Good Ol' Boy Theater* has become a popular bit on our show and is really what got the whole Rick and Bubba phenomenon started in the first place. (We call it a phenomenon because we're getting to do what we love, are having a lot of fun in the process, and we get paid for it. Can you think of a more accurate description of a *phenomenon*?) Instead of reading Shakespeare, as co-president, I (Bubba) will read from the national budget. That ought to be good for some laughs.

One more favorite radio bit that we do is a take-off on all the endurance reality shows. We call it *Rick and Bubba's Real Survivor*. For all of you *Survivor* fans, we're going to level with you: We don't think it is truly "surviving" when you are in the wilderness with a full television crew, fourteen equipment trucks, and a fully stocked craft services truck nearby. That sounds more like a film shoot to us.

What we do on our radio show is *real* survival. We put someone in a locked-off room at the studio with no food, no cell phone, and no restroom facilities, and then we see how long he can endure *that*.

We would like to continue doing this feature on our radio show from the White House, only we would call it *Rick and Bubba's Congress Survival*. The thinking behind it is this: You know how Congress will sometimes filibuster a bill? That can really slow things down on Capitol Hill, can't it? But we wonder how quickly they would take care of the country's business and pass a good bill if they were locked in their chambers and not given any food or water or any modern conveniences until they could come to an agreement. There would be none of this, "We're going on vacation. We'll take care of that bill when we get back." They would have to stay in that room and talk it out until the bill is either approved or voted down. Just think of all the work they could get done under those circumstances.

Another bit that we do is called *The Running of the Goobs*. Goobs are what we respectfully call our radio consultants or program directors. And "Goob" is an endearing word that is short for, well, "Goober." Being diehard Andy Griffith fans, the word *Goober* is always meant as a compliment.

The Running of the Goobs usually takes place on my (Rick) birthday. At the designated time, the Goobs are let loose to run through the woods, and we get to shoot at them with a paint gun. It's all good, harmless fun, and you wouldn't believe how much pent-up frustration it releases for all of us at the radio station.

From time to time during our weekly presidential radio broadcast, we'll hold *The Running of the Congress*. We might even make it part of the White House tour. At the designated time, Congress will run across the White House lawn, and as they do, the president, his cabinet, and selected tourists will have the opportunity to shoot paintballs at them. It would be sort of like a shooting gallery, only instead of hitting a vulture, turkey, or a dodo bird every few shots, you'd hit a . . . okay, bad example.

The Congress wouldn't be dressed in camo either. We would want to see them running in their regular suits, while we yell out reminders like, "You're a public servant! You're a public servant!"

We have no idea how much pent-up frustration of the president, his staff, and even average American citizens could be released by an official event like this. But we're willing to give it a try.

Probably the best thing about doing a radio show from the White House would be having a twenty-four-hour chef at our disposal. To us, that would be about as close to heaven as we could imagine. How cool would it be to just declare "I want a peanut butter and jelly sandwich," and then have someone bring it to you? The president of the United States has that kind of power. He could have a peanut-butter-and-jelly-sandwich phone, like the red phone, if he wanted it. Then, all he'd have to do is pick up the PB & J phone, and the sandwich would appear. Like magic. That's power. We don't have that kind of power at the radio station now. We usually have to make our own sandwiches, or send out for them.

Maybe that's the whole reason why we're running for co-presidency—unlimited peanut butter and jelly sandwiches. It could very well be the real reason a lot of other candidates are running, too.

THE FAA

If we are elected co-presidents, there is no way that the following would ever happen over America's skies.

It seems a passenger who was seated in the first-class section on a flight from New Delhi to London woke up from a nap to find that someone had moved, or more accurately, had been moved, to the seat next to him. He didn't mind so much that his sleeping space had just been invaded, and it wasn't that the fellow passenger was unusually obnoxious. What he did mind was that his fellow passenger was a corpse. Apparently, the poor woman had died in the economy section of the airplane and had been bumped up to first class for the duration of the flight. (We've always wondered what you had to do to get upgraded to first class.)

The airline moved the body to the front of the plane to cause the least amount of commotion. (How it got past the serving tray with no commotion is beyond us.)

There was some turbulence during the flight, so the body had to be strapped in next to the napping man to keep it in place. Without any natural resistance, however, the body apparently kept slipping down out of the seat belt with every bump and jerk. Finally, the body had to be wedged in place with an armful of airline pillows. (That's the saddest part. It's bad

31

enough to be dead, but to be laid to rest on those uncomfortable airline pillows is downright pitiful.)

According to a spokesman for the airline, about ten passengers die each year while airborne. In one way, that is kind of a cool way to go. You'd already be about thirty-eight thousand feet closer to heaven.

The airlines say there is no way for them to anticipate these rare and unexpected in-flight deaths. Each case has to be handled on an individual basis with as much respect for the deceased as possible.

When we were apprised of these facts about our aviation system (presidents are always being apprised of things, so we're practicing), we decided we had to come up with a solution for dealing with these situations.

The problem is not easily solved. When you think about it, what else could the airline staff have done in this instance? They couldn't move the body to the cockpit with the pilots. Since 9/11, no one except authorized personnel is allowed in there, dead or alive. And they couldn't put the body in one of the lavatories. The line for one of those is usually long enough as it is. They couldn't buckle the body in one of the emergency row seats because the person wouldn't meet the most basic criteria for sitting there: to be breathing. The overhead compartments are out because everyone knows they're already packed to the brim.

No, after careful deliberation, we decided that the flight attendants chose the best option they had at the time—to move the deceased passenger up to the first-class section. It wasn't as crowded up there, and no one ever complains about being upgraded to first class. In fact, the deceased's relatives might be comforted to know their loved one had gone out in style. Had that guy whose nap was disturbed by the dead woman sitting next to him really thought about it, he would have counted his blessings. At least the woman didn't talk his ear off for the duration of the flight. It's all in how you look at things. We assure you, though, if we are the ultimate authority over our nation's airlines, we will make sure that a regular plan of action is in place for this sort of thing. Not only for when a person dies in flight, but for when a person dies while on the phone at home waiting to make an airline reservation.

Another thing that we would change about the airlines is their food. Or lack of it. One of the most puzzling questions of our time is this: What happened to airline food? Sure, we used to make fun of it, and some of us passed on it even when it was offered. But at least we had the choice. Now what do we get? Pretzels—or even worse, peanuts. Did any of you ask for peanuts? We know we didn't. What's next? Mini-rice cakes? You can't tell us that an airline that charges some $300–600 per ticket can't do better than peanuts. When we fly from Nashville to New York, we want more than peanuts. When we fly from Atlanta to Los Angeles, we want more than four pretzels. When we fly from Birmingham to Orlando, we want more than a biscotti cracker. Sure, they're good, but we want more.

That's why, under our administration, it will be mandated that every passenger flying an hour or more will receive at least a sandwich and some chips. This would be a *real* sandwich, too. Not one that you make out of Ritz crackers and salami. We're talking a sandwich that would require more than one bite to consume. (We have been known to eat a Big Mac in one bite on occasion, but you know what we mean.) A sandwich with real bread and real meat.

Some airlines are still offering meals, but now they're charging you for it. You order from your seat. When it is your turn, you have to repeat your order two or three times because they can't hear you. Then, when you're finally convinced they heard you order the turkey sandwich, they take your money and hand you the chicken salad with no dressing. Sound a bit like dinner in the drive-thru lane?

I (Rick) might not mind the peanuts and pretzels so much if the flights would just leave on time. If I am going to be sitting at the gate in an airplane with no air conditioning for over two hours, my body at least needs a club sandwich. Or three or four.

When we're in charge, there will be no more overbooking of flights either. We do not understand this practice. What kind of madness is this concept of selling more seats than you have, hoping that all the passengers don't show up? Can you imagine the riots that would break out if the Super Bowl did this? Or rock concerts?

This practice, aside from inciting riots, is turning the airlines into seat scalpers. "Hey, we'll give someone a hotel and three hundred dollars worth of tickets if you'll get off the plane." I'm sure there are people who buy tickets on popular flights and stand around at the airport just waiting for the best offer (that's how Bubba and I plan to fund our retirement), but it does complicate matters at the airports.

The airlines also need to start enforcing the "Bin-Hog Rule." When someone attempts to carry on a standup bass and stuff it into the overhead compartment, something has got to be said.

Another rule we would enforce is no more alcohol being served during the flight. It's bad enough being trapped at a football or baseball stadium with a bunch of drunks. Do we really have to have the inebriated riding with us in close quarters at thirty thousand feet in a pressurized tube?

And getting back to the pillows—we're sorry, but airline pillows really have to go. Why are we asked to relax on the same size pillow a Yorkshire terrier would keep in his basket? We're not Yorkshire terriers. They may be serving us doggie biscuits for lunch, but we're not dogs.

We also believe that parachutes should be issued to each and every passenger. When the flight attendant goes over the FAA rules during the taxi to the runway, are we the only ones who think the part about the magic life-saving seat cushion is a waste of time? Are they telling us that our only safety gear is what we're sitting on? How's that supposed to break our fall from thirty thousand feet? Sure, it's made to float if we land in the ocean, but think about it. If you're heading into the Atlantic at five hundred miles per hour, is a seat cushion the size of a backpack really going to save you?

Our co-presidency is about solving real life problems. Give us parachutes. Now that's something we could use. And some sandwiches.

A TAXING SITUATION

The Rick and Bubba tax plan is a simple one, and it is one more thing that sets us apart from our competition. Our plan is a straight 10 percent tax across the board. If 10 percent is good enough for God, it should be good enough for the government of the nation under God. If we're all having to tighten our belts (and that's something that has never come easy to either one of us), then why can't Washington do the same?

The Rick and Bubba 10 Percent Flat Tax Plan works like this—if your household income is $20,000 a year, your tax would be 10 percent of $20,000, which is $2,000. If you make $4,000,000 a year (say, you're a rock star or really good at playing Bingo), your tax would be 10 percent of $4,000,000, which is $400,000. Now if you're anywhere near as smart as a fifth grader, you'll be able to do the math and realize that $400,000 is a lot more tax than $2,000. That's what makes the tax fair. The rich are being taxed at the same percentage as the rest of us, but because their base is higher, their tax is higher. In other words, the more you make, the more you pay. The less you make, the less you pay. And no one is exempt. Under our plan everyone pays. That way, everyone would be invested in the system. If you only make ten dollars on your paper route, your tax is a buck. With this plan, Washington should end up with more than enough money to pay its bills.

It will probably never happen, though. Why? Because it makes sense. Ideas that make sense sometimes have a hard time getting through the channels in Washington.

Also, whenever the government finds itself with more than enough money to pay its bills, it will usually find a way to increase spending so we'll have a deficit again. It's like us paying off our VISA cards, then going right out and charging them up again. Many of us do this on a regular basis, but we don't want our government doing it, especially when we're the ones having to pay all their monthly payments.

The Rick and Bubba Tax Plan would have provisions in it to guard against this type of fiscal irresponsibility. Anyone promoting a new government program that comes with any kind of significant price tag would have to answer the following three questions before any money is spent:

1. Do we need it?
2. Do we need it?
3. Do we need it?

If the answer to all three questions is "No," then the program will not be funded. Simple as that. I (Rick) use this kind of decision-making style in my family all the time.

"Dad, can I buy a new car?"
"No. We don't have the money."

"Dad, can I go to the concert Friday night?"
"No. We don't have the money."

"How do you like my new hunting rifle, Sherri?"
"I thought I told you we didn't have the money."
"It was on sale. There wasn't time to call for a vote."

Now, some people have complained that a flat tax would put a lot of accountants out of business since it would only take the average person about twenty minutes to do his or her taxes. But we say, *And your point is . . .* ? Besides, if the accountants run out of things to do, they can help all of us who trusted in Social Security find another way to fund our retirements.

Another reason why we want the flat tax is because it evens things out. The way things are set up now, our country is slowly turning into a caste system. Rich people are depicted as evil, poor people as lazy, and the middle class keeps getting stuck paying all the bills. This isn't how it should be.

Let's start with the rich people. Do you know that most rich people are not evil? Some may be. Some may have made their fortune from sticking it to the common man, but the majority of them are just hard-working Americans whose dedication and work ethic paid off. Think about it—a rich person probably gave you your job. A rich person gave us our jobs, too. Rich people own the restaurants we go to and the stores where we buy our groceries. Your neighbor, the one driving that twenty-year-old clunker to work everyday, may be rich. Rich people don't always look like rich people. They don't always live in Beverly Hills and drive BMWs, either.

Whoever they are, wherever they live, rich people are good for America. We happen to love rich people. They've taken a lot of us along with them on their ride to fortune. They've been our mentors and have put bread on our tables and clothes on our backs.

If elected, we aim to start a "Hug a Rich Person" day. It's fitting. Rich people have set an example of where hard work and a sense of purpose can take anyone who wants to put forth the effort.

On the other side of the coin (no pun intended), poor people aren't necessarily lazy either. There could be a lot of different reasons why someone is poor. ATM fees and the price of gas are just two of them.

Now, let's talk about the middle class. The real reason that the middle class keeps getting stuck with the bill is that when the check comes, we usually look around and if no one else is volunteering to pick up the tab, we say, "I'll take that." Instead of letting everyone pay their own fair share, we keep picking up the tab by default. We have a voice; we just don't always use it. We have a vote, but sometimes election night interferes with *American Idol*. You've got to put blame where blame belongs, and sometimes it belongs with us.

Just who is considered rich and who is viewed as poor could be a matter of skewed statistics, too. Have you noticed that when a candidate is running for office, the figures on the nation's "poor" suddenly swell to include people at your own income level? Then, once the person's in office and feels the need to pump up the figures on the nation's "rich," your same income figure is moved over to the rich column and is then used to justify a tax increase on the "rich." How does that make sense? You're still living on the same money you've always lived on. But one day you are poor, and the next you are rich? Kind of makes you want whoever's in charge to leave your wallet alone so you can get on with your life, doesn't it?

We realize we need some sort of tax system so that our country can run smoothly, but let's make it simple and easy to follow, and above all else, fair. Don't play around with the statistics like we're stupid. We're a nation of educated people. Most of us passed math.

They try to do the same funny math with your home. For tax purposes, they will appraise your house for a higher value. Then, when you go to a lending institution and try to get a loan on that amount, the lender will say your home is worth less than the tax assessor's office said, and they won't lend on it.

Since the vast majority of us are middle class, why are we putting up with this sort of treatment?

Go back and reread that last sentence. Never mind, we'll repeat it for you. *Since the vast majority of us are middle class, why are we putting up with this sort of treatment?* We need to unite and tell those in charge that we're mad as you-know-what and we're not going to take it anymore. If Washington doesn't start meeting more of our demands (such as better wages, less taxes, and whatever amount of fat we want in our diet), we'll go on strike! You watch us! Why, we'll . . .

All right, who are we kidding? The middle class would never go on strike. We're over our limit on our fourteen credit cards, and three payments behind on our Excursion and high-definition television sets. We need our money too bad to quit paying so much in taxes.

And somehow that makes sense to us!

Then, there's the credit crunch. Anyone with half a brain had to have seen this coming. People were rushing out and getting $500,000 loans on a paperboy income. It doesn't take a mathematical genius to see that this was going to be a problem somewhere down the road. I don't so much blame the paperboy; after all, who wouldn't want a $500,000 home? (Note: The same paperboy in California would have a former meth lab in a bad neighborhood for $500,000—though it's worth $80,000 anywhere else—but that's Arnold's problem.)

Realtors, loan officers, and escrow companies were having a field day making money off of these kinds of loans. Now apparently, it's time to pay the piper. But who do you think the government wants to pay for bailing us out of this credit mess? You got it—the middle class.

Don't even get us started on credit card companies. With interest rates at 16 percent, 24 percent, 28 percent, and climbing, where is their conscience? Some credit card companies are making loan sharks look honest. Do these companies think that no one is paying attention to what they're doing? It's like they're stealing second base and hoping the other team won't notice. But we're looking right at them. We read their letters announcing their rate increases. We see it printed on our monthly statements. We even know what APR means—"A Permissible Robbery." But we still pay it. Month after month after month.

What's the matter with us? Are we so addicted to living above our means that we'll just keep whipping out the plastic and digging our hole deeper and deeper? Raising our monthly payments wasn't the answer. Maybe it was for the credit card companies, but it just put most of the cardholders behind, where the banks could then charge another $29 late fee, which bumps the account over its credit limit by four cents so they can tack on another $39 over-the-limit fee. How is this helping the consumer? (Remember when we said some of the rich are evil? These people might fall under that category.)

Not long ago, I (Rick) mailed in the final payment on one of my credit cards. A little over a month later, I received another statement in the mail saying that I owed an additional $35. I called to see why, and they explained to me that because I "missed" the following month's payment (I was short a few dollars on the payoff, but I was under the assumption that I had paid it in full and didn't need to make any more payments), I was hit with a late fee. I now owed them a late charge of $35, plus the remaining couple of dollars balance on my account.

All I could say to the man was, "How do you sleep at night?"

Now, when I pay off a credit card, I overpay by about a dollar. Then I let the credit card company send me statements stating that "No payment is due at this time" for about nine or ten months. After I feel they've wasted enough postage and personnel hours managing my overpaid account, I write and ask them to mail me a check for the balance on my account. In three equal payments. I figure that much bookkeeping has got to be costing them something. It's not much revenge, but it helps *me* sleep a little better at night.

THE STEPHEN COLBERT FACTOR

We feel our strongest competition is Stephen Colbert. The other candidates can compete for the serious vote. But for that disgruntled, dissatisfied, disenfranchised, discontented, unhappy, angry, annoyed, disillusioned, peeved, disheartened, cynical, distrustful, skeptical voter, Stephen Colbert is our closest competitor.

We like Stephen. His persona is clever, witty, and ultraconservative. So why is he running on the Democratic ticket? This makes no sense, and of course, that's what makes him a perfect candidate.

Seriously, it is our understanding that the reason Stephen Colbert is running (at least at the time of this book's printing) on the Democratic ticket is that in South Carolina, his home state, it is cheaper to file candidacy papers as a Democrat than it is to file as a Republican. It was, in fact, a matter of $2,500 versus $35,000. If that's right, that's enough of a difference to tempt even us to switch parties.

But once again, instead of going that far, we're trying to bypass all the paperwork and run as a write-in candidate.

There are other differences between Stephen Colbert and us besides the Republican vs. Democrat factor. You may not have noticed, but Stephen Colbert is thinner than we are. This may not seem like an important factor to you, but think about it. Can you truly trust someone as thin as Stephen

Colbert not to insult the leaders of foreign countries by refusing to take seconds, thirds, and in some cases even fourths of the food offered to him at their formal dinners? Wars have broken out over insults smaller than this. Every extra pound we carry was gained as a result of trying not to hurt someone's feelings. We have sacrificed our bodies for the cause of peace and harmony. Can Stephen Colbert say that?

Also, Colbert is only running in one state—South Carolina. We are open to being written in on the ballot in all fifty states. And maybe even Canada. Who's being inclusive now?

Stephen Colbert has also been quoted as saying that he really doesn't want to be president. He just wants to run for the office. See, that's where we differ again. If elected, we wouldn't mind moving to the White House and being the new leaders of the greatest country in the free world. Not that we're on a power trip or anything like that. We just like the idea of "Hail to the Chief" being played every time we walk into a room. (We've tried to get our wives to do that now, but so far they haven't cooperated.)

Stephen has also changed his name from Colbert (pronounced Colbert) to Colbert (pronounced Col-bair). Don't you think that's a little odd? What is he hiding? We have not changed our names. They have and will always be Rick (pronounced Rick) and Bubba (pronounced Buh-buh).

Probably the biggest difference between Stephen Colbert and us is that there is only one of him. With us, it's a two-for-one special. We realize this is a new concept, but as we've been pointing out throughout this book, it does have plenty of advantages. The best one is if you don't like one of your presidents, you still have another one to respect.

A comedian running for president isn't anything new, either. *Laugh In*'s Pat Paulsen did it in the 1960s. Bob Hope did it a couple of times on his television specials. Other comedians have done it, too. Comedian Dick Gregory did it for real in 1968.

So none of us are blazing new trails here. America has had comedians on the campaign trail before. A comedian hasn't won yet, but some of the politicians who did make it to the White House ended up giving us plenty of laughs.

We wish the best of luck to Stephen Colbert. We can't say we'll vote for him (we need every vote for ourselves), but if he does somehow end up winning the presidency, we'll accept our loss graciously.

And immediately start the recount.

GOVERNMENT
ON A DIET

We know we griped about America's whole-grain obsession with all things low-carb earlier, but there is one area where we are adamantly pro-diet: the government. We don't just believe in a small government. We believe in a tiny government. We want our government to be the size of a gnat. We are going to do everything in our power to make Congress live within its means.

The government spends too much money, and for the most part it spends money it doesn't have. We may be just a couple of boys from Alabama, but we passed ninth-grade algebra our senior year of high school, and we know the principle of if you only make $2, it doesn't mean you have $3 to spend. That's just common sense, isn't it?

For years our government has needed to be on a diet. No matter how much it consumes, it can never get enough. Every time you feed it, it comes back for more. And more. And more.

One area where Washington could start trimming the fat is all those fancy White House dinners. Do we really need to continue having so many of those? They are expensive, and in some instances a complete waste of money because they're for dignitaries we don't even like.

To save money, why don't we give the five-star chef the night off and just offer foreign dignitaries who happen to drop by a meat and three instead? (For you non-Southerners, a "meat and three" is one entrée and three side

43

choices, two of which are usually gravy. It's not prime rib, but it's adequate nutrition that won't break the bank.) We're a super power, for goodness's sake. We don't need to be wasting money on all this protocol and presentation. Martha Stewart isn't running this country. Foreign leaders who are our friends will be fine with whatever kind of meal we serve them. Foreign leaders who are our enemies will stay our enemies no matter how good the dinner is. Bringing out the good china isn't going to put an enemy in a better mood. I doubt if Mahmoud Ahmadinejad would say, "These are the most beautiful dishes I have ever seen! Cancel our nuclear program at once!"

To save money on housekeeping and maintenance, we might even do away with the White House dining room altogether. We don't think it's necessary. Who eats in the dining room anymore? In most homes it's a museum that you only enter once or twice a year.

So instead of paying for the upkeep on the White House dining room, we will invite our dinner guests to eat off a card table, or even better, on the sofa in front of the television set. We're sure the Queen of England won't mind if the situation was explained to her correctly. The Queen's all for saving money. She must be.

Do you really think she pays top dollar for all those hats?

GETTING OUT THE VOTE

Each of the candidates has his or her own way of getting out the vote on Election Day. We do too: *free food.* If we have learned anything over the years, we have learned this: free food works. Actually, free *anything* works. If you want a crowd to show up at an event, just announce that you'll be giving away free stuff and they'll turn out in droves. (We've told our fans that there will be free CDs distributed at each of our funerals, and so far the RSVPs have been tremendous.)

That's how we plan to get out the vote this November. No, not by dying. We're not that committed. We are going to give away free stuff. Lots of free stuff. But it won't be government cheese. We've felt your pain—we know free cheese isn't much without free chips and salsa, too. When we say food giveaways, we're talking about full meals. Barbeques. Big barbeques. We're thinking about roasting a whole pig at every whistle stop. Think about it— we'll be out on the campaign trail trying to put an end to government pork, and we'll all be eating pork. How fitting is that?

We will also offer to pick up voters and bus them to the precincts on Election Day ourselves . . . whether they want to go or not. Some people may look upon this as kidnapping, but it isn't really. Not in the technical sense. We're simply offering a service. We'll even assign a voting assistant to every-one in Broward County, Florida, so there won't be any more chad problems.

One thing we won't be doing is calling you at home during dinner. We hate that sort of thing, and we're pretty sure you do, too. There's nothing more frustrating than sitting down with your family for a plate of franks and beans, only to have some politician call and tell you how much better the economy would be if you'd just re-elect him or her.

We refuse to interrupt your dinner hour. We realize that dinner time is one of the most important times of the day, outside of breakfast and lunch. (And maybe brunch.) And being the savvy political strategists we are, why would we call your house and interrupt your meal just to get your vote? That could backfire on us and make you so mad that you'll vote for our opponent just to get even. If it's dinnertime and we get an overwhelming desire to try to convince some of you to vote for us, we're not going to stop you from eating with a phone call. We're going to just pop on over and eat *with* you.

So save us some biscuits.

PRESS CONFERENCES

Some classic moments have happened before a microphone. Who can forget the time when President Ronald Reagan didn't realize that his microphone was on and during a sound check said, "My fellow Americans, I'm pleased to tell you today that I've signed legislation that will outlaw Russia forever. We begin bombing in five minutes." (That's what we loved about President Reagan. Not only was he a brilliant and fearless leader, but he had a great sense of humor.)

It may sound strange, but we are actually looking forward to holding press conferences, doing weekly radio addresses, and dealing with the Washington press corps.

From what we can tell, they're too stuffy and can use a few more laughs.

We're thinking about opening our press conferences with some funny comments about current events, you know, like Jay Leno, David Letterman, Johnny Carson, and other great entertainers do. Our thinking is that since some members of the press seem to enjoy having so many laughs at the president's expense, why not beat them to the punch line, so to speak, and do our own jokes on the issue first?

After the monologue, we could open the conference up for questions. The press corps might not always like what we have to say, but we are going to tell it like it is. We're Baptists and aren't allowed to dance, even if it is only around an issue.

Also, since we're both in the radio talk show business, we're already used to stating our opinions. It will be easy for us to step up to take charge of the interview by saying something like, "It's time for a break now. Where are the refreshments?"

We have often felt sorry for people like Tony Snow and other White House spokespersons who, in the past, have had to face some fairly hostile reporters who haven't shown a lot of respect for the office of the president. We don't believe this is right. No matter what someone's political leaning happens to be, the office of the president of the United States deserves respect. Even when we don't agree with the actions of the person in office, the office itself should be respected. So if we're elected and a reporter shows disdain for the office, he or she will be promptly invited to leave the White House grounds. Once we get the catapult built (one of our executive privileges), that process will go quicker. Or better yet, maybe we'll just take the Donald Rumsfeld approach during press conferences, and whenever the office is shown disrespect we'll just say, "That's a stupid question. Next."

We understand that the press needs to do its job, too. We also realize that once we take that oath of office, much of our privacy will have to be surrendered. If we happen to burp, it'll be on the evening news. Like when George Bush, Sr. lost his cookies at that dinner with those Japanese dignitaries. It made the cover of magazines and newspapers all over the world. The poor guy got sick (sushi can sometimes do that to you), and the photographers captured it all on film.

(Note to Presidential Press Corps: If that ever happens to us at a dinner, offer us a towel and a Tums before you start snapping pictures, okay?)

Being in the public eye is nothing new to us, though. Because of our radio show, we can't tell you how many times we've gone out to dinner with our families and someone has come up to us, camera in hand, and interrupted our meal. Even after we strike a pose and they hand us a camera and ask us to take a photo of their party, we're more than happy to oblige.

We've got that public servant concept down pat.

CAMPAIGN PROMISES

We promise to make only one campaign promise, and that's to not make any campaign promises. None, nada, zip, zero. Ours will be the only honest bumper sticker of the entire presidential campaign: *"Rick and Bubba—We promise you absolutely nothing!"* How could we possibly lose with that kind of a pledge? One thing's for sure, anything we accomplish will be gravy.

After all, we all know that a campaign promise can get a candidate into hot water when it isn't carried out. Remember George Bush, Sr.'s promise of "Read my lips—no new taxes"? He fell for the trap set by the "We have to raise taxes, or life as we know it will come to an end" crowd. When he changed his mind and eventually raised taxes, these same people never let him live it down. They reminded him of his campaign promise and claimed he wasn't a man of his word.

The moral of the story? When you tell people to read your lips, make sure your lips are saying what you want them to be saying, not just what someone else wants you to say. That's why it's not a good idea to make any campaign promises in the first place. We don't want people reading our lips. We'd rather them read our books and leave our lips alone.

The main problem with campaign promises is the fact that candidates set goals too high. They'll say anything just to get elected, but then when they get into office, they realize their promises are almost impossible to achieve, so they discard them. They may have had the best of intentions, but good intentions depend on too many unpredictable factors, like Congress. Candidates should keep this in mind when making their campaign promises, and tweak them in such a way that they'll be a lot easier to keep. Presidents are judged by the number of their promises that they keep.

For example, instead of promising voters the moon, a candidate should offer more attainable goals, such as:

"I promise to see to it that our nation's bridges are repaired . . . sometime."

"I promise to fix Social Security . . . before *I* need it."

"I promise to cut the crime rate by half . . . or by some other fraction."

"I promise to do all I can to lower the price of gas . . . at least at one gas station in America. Most likely, in my hometown."

"I promise to improve education. I shall appoint a spell-check committee over graffiti."

"I promise to be strong on defense . . . in my Fantasy Football game."

"I promise to increase the minimum wage . . . before I retire and end up a Wal-Mart greeter."

"I promise to be open and forthright with the American public . . . unless there's a good reason not to be."

"I promise to improve our nation's health care. Free aspirin for every American on the night of my State of the Union address."

"I promise that the pursuit of peace will be my number one goal . . . I'm going to do everything my wife tells me to do."

See how easy it would be to keep promises like these? There is no need for a candidate to go out on a limb and make pledges that might not be kept.

Or better yet, all the candidates should be more like us and not make any promises at all.

A FEW CHANGES

The first change we would make to our country has to do with the topic of re-election. We realize that if we're fortunate enough to get elected, this problem won't even come up for another four years, but as we said, we like to think ahead. Besides, this is an important issue that really needs to be addressed from day one because it could potentially save the nation a ton of money. We're talking, of course, about second inaugural parties.

If we are re-elected to a second term, we will not, we repeat, we will NOT be throwing a second inaugural party. The first oath should still cover us, and it seems like a complete waste of government money to have another ceremony and celebration. I (Rick) have to agree with my brother, Greg Burgess, on this one. As he so wisely put it in our last book, the first oath of office should stay in force until a president physically moves out of the White House. As long as he or she is living there, the same rules of the first term should apply. You don't go through the expense of a wedding every anniversary just to tell your spouse you're giving him or her "another year," right? You can do that if you want to, but it isn't required. The original vows still apply.

Another change that we would make is to get Ted Kennedy off the government payroll. It's nothing against Ted personally, and it has nothing to do with his age. It doesn't even have to do with his politics. He's just been there long enough. We would like a little more variety on our evening news.

Why do we have to keep seeing the same faces, Republican or Democrat? We practically memorized every wrinkle on Strom Thurmond's face by the time he left (and we see Robert Byrd's face in our dreams sometimes—believe us, it's not fun). Our presidents can only stay a maximum of eight years, and after that, in most cases, they're out of the public eye. They may show up at some photo op every now and then, or fly off to a foreign country to have brunch with its leader. But they're not on the evening news on a regular basis. Why can't the rest of Washington do the same? We say, serve your time and then get on with your regular life.

We might need to form a committee to see how we can legally and respectfully get some of these "lifers" to leave their government jobs. Some of them are pretty entrenched in the system, and we may need a Jaws of Life to pry them away. We may even have to change the locks on the Senate or House chambers, sort of like what landlords do when you're evicted. We're still working out the details.

Now hear us on this one: We're not saying that these politicians are not doing a good job, or that they're not nice people. It's just time to let someone else have a turn. That's one of the first things you learn as a child, isn't it? You've got to take turns. It's like waiting at an amusement park ride and then having the person who just got off immediately cut in line in front of everyone else to take another ride. We don't want to hear you tell us what a fun or harrowing ride it was. Let some of the rest of us find that out for ourselves. *It's time to get off the ride!*

Let us assure you, though, that even if we have to use legal congressional eviction notices, we'll give them all nice parting gifts.

FIRST PETS

There will be no pets in the White House during our administration. Not that we don't love animals. We do. But having a pet usually involves potty training, and it has long been our belief that the words "White House" and "potty training" should never be used in the same sentence. No president should have to chase a creature around the White House scolding him about the proper place to do his "business." Didn't we have enough of that sort of thing with Billy Carter?

Sorry if it disappoints some of our supporters, but you will not be seeing us stepping off Air Force One with a puppy in our arms. All of our family pets will be left at home in Alabama with someone in charge of feeding and bathing them. Other than a couple of hunting dogs kept in a dog cage on the White House lawn until quail season, there will be no animals in our administration.

Frankly, we have never understood why the leader of the free world would step off Air Force One with a puppy in his arms anyway. It's hard enough to walk down those airplane ramp steps without falling (remember Gerald Ford?). So why would a president put life and limb at risk just to be photographed carrying the family dog? Doesn't holding a poodle diminish the aura of the most powerful man in the world? Could it possibly be that he feels more comfortable with the dog because it's doing less growling and biting than the Washington press corps?

We know we'll get letters from animal lovers across the nation, but we're adamant on this one. No pets for us in the White House. We've never liked keeping pets in the house period, much less 1600 Pennsylvania Avenue. In our opinion, pets don't belong indoors. Some people try to speak for them and say how much their pet loves being inside the house. But if they like it so much, why are they always trying to get out every time the door is opened?

The biggest problem with having a presidential pet is that they can sometimes get a bigger book advance than you do. Remember George and Barbara's dog, Millie? Did Millie even invite them to the book release party?

Then, there was Socks, Bill and Hillary Clinton's cat. Cats are a completely different story altogether. You can have a dog in the White House and maybe get by with people not noticing. But never a cat. It's impossible not to notice a cat in the house. Even if the house has 132 rooms to hide in, a cat will make his or her presence known. It's the litter box issue. We've never understood litter boxes ourselves. Think about it—if someone knocked on your door with a box of cat droppings and asked if they could bring it into your home, would you let them? But some people will keep a litter box in the corner of our family rooms and tell everyone who will listen how much cleaner cats are than dogs.

But again, let us make ourselves clear. We have nothing against what other presidents have done. This is just our own personal policy. There will not be any animals in the White House during our administration.

Except maybe for a few snakes that happen to slither down from Congress.

FIRST LADIES

When voting for president, it is important to consider what kind of first lady (or first husband) the candidate will be bringing along to the White House. As a country, we have learned the hard way that when we elect a president, we get the spouse, too. It's like the marriage ceremony. You may be marrying one person, but the whole dysfunctional family comes along with the package. (We say dysfunctional because all families are a bit dysfunctional. No matter how perfect we may think our family is. Dysfunctional families go back all the way to the days of Adam and Eve and their sons Cain and Abel. One kid killed the other kid out of jealousy, and there wasn't even a PlayStation 3 to fight over. So none of us should be too pious when it comes to a politician's family. All family trees have their share of broken and bent branches. And maybe even a few nuts.)

Still, since the first lady has the president's ear much of the time, voters are wise to keep that in mind when they step into the voting booth and start punching out those chads. The first lady or first husband's name may not be on the ballot, but believe us, that person is an important influence and is part of the ticket.

We feel our wives, Betty and Sherri, will make wonderful first ladies. First of all, they won't be wasting any time or money picking out new china. Eleanor Roosevelt's dishes are good enough for them. Besides, don't you think the First Lady of the free world has bigger issues to worry about than new china? Betty and Sherri will just use Eleanor's dishes and put the rest of the china sets on eBay to try to make a little extra money for the country.

I (Bubba) have to say that America could do a lot worse than having Betty Bussey as its first lady. If we want to go back to being loved and respected by the world, Betty is one who could pull that off. Her natural charm will win over even our toughest critics.

Her nursing skills would come in handy, too, especially if I ever choke on a pretzel, or go on a hunting trip with Dick Cheney.

There's one other thing. And I'm not just saying this because I'm married to her and I prefer sleeping *inside* the house. But Betty is about as fine-looking a woman as can be. I realize this isn't necessarily a requirement of a first lady (we refer again to Eleanor Roosevelt), but beauty can sure be a plus. Let's be honest, it doesn't matter what history has gone on between nations, what the language barriers are, or what the current tensions happen to be—the whole world recognizes a fine woman. Greeting a fine woman has to put foreign dignitaries in a better mood. And Betty, in her husband's humble opinion, is off-the-chart fine.

She's funny too. When Betty goes into a fit of laughter after getting tickled over something, people at airports or wherever we happen to be, people who don't even know Betty, will start gathering around just to hear her laugh. She has one of those contagious laughs, the kind of laugh that when you hear it, you just can't help but laugh along yourself.

Wouldn't it be nice to see Kim Jong Il and Mahmoud Ahmadinejad getting tickled over something Betty has said? Those two look like they haven't had a good laugh in years.

Betty's mission as first lady would be to remind the world that laughter is universal. When they can laugh with their neighboring countries, they don't have to invade them. When we can all laugh together, discussions about the dangers of nuclear proliferation might come a little easier. As long as we can laugh, and understand the importance of working toward a common goal of world peace and human rights for all, there is no reason for us to bomb each other off the planet.

I (Rick) agree that Betty would be a welcomed and wonderful addition to the White House.

The same goes for my wife, Sherri. I'm not just saying that because we need their votes, either (although it would be a travesty to lose the election by only two votes).

The truth of the matter is Betty and Sherri deserve to have their portraits hanging in the White House. They are both beautiful women. Mrs. Bush is a very attractive lady, too. She's a first lady that we can be proud of. But let's be perfectly honest here, with the exception of Laura Bush, Jacqueline Kennedy Onassis, and a few others, you have to go back pretty far before reaching another one that measures up. Maybe they were all intelligent women, but some of them were a little tough on the eyes, if you know what I mean. Not that you have to be pretty to be a first lady. That's not what I'm saying. It's just that sometimes you luck out and get both beauty and intelligence in one package, and I believe Sherri and Betty are that package.

Our wives are feminine, too. They're comfortable in their femininity. Sherri doesn't have any desire to act like a man. She used to work in radio and television and can hold her own in almost any situation, so we're not talking "the weaker sex" here. We're talking a confident, beautiful woman who treats femininity as an asset, not a curse.

Somewhere Sherri came up with the bizarre concept that men and women are different (even before the government-funded study reached the same conclusion) and that it's okay to capitalize on those differences. Imagine that.

Sherri's experience in the media should also help her with presidential news conferences. She won't simply stand by my side and look up at me adoringly. As much as I'd like that (and if I remember correctly, it was part of our wedding vows), she is her own person and will have her own work to do once we move to Washington. First ladies usually have their pet projects, such as education, health care, child advocacy, or drug awareness, and Sherri will be no different. Sherri's passion is to get America to turn back to our Judeo-Christian heritage and once again honor God, country, and family.

First off, she would do everything in her power to bring prayer back to our schools. She is passionate about this. And pretty convincing. If given the chance, Sherri could persuade even the biggest skeptic that when prayer went out of our public school system, the atmosphere on our campuses started changing—and not for the better, either. But Sherri wants to change that downward slide. According to Sherri, if one woman could get prayer taken out of our schools, then one woman can get it put back in. Sherri wants to be that woman. And we agree with her cause. Bubba and I always prayed at our schools. Especially during tests. Many say it's the only reason we graduated.

Sherri would also have very little tolerance for crazy foreign leaders. She might listen to a rant or two, but then she'd stop and say to herself, "Why am I talking to this idiot?" (Sherri has never been one to mince words.) To Sherri, it is black and white—if you are an enemy of our country, she won't act like you're a friend. When someone says "Death to America," Sherri doesn't hear "Kumbaya."

If Sherri has to eat dinner with the wife of an enemy dictator, things could turn ugly. Before the evening is over she will probably end up asking her, "Why are you married to this dufus?" Her aim would not be to start World War III, or even to cause the woman to leave her husband. It's just Sherri's way of defending America. She'll defend our kids and me the same way. She has our back. When it comes to her country and those she loves, diplomacy has never been Sherri's strong point. But that's all right; we have ambassadors for that.

Sherri would also save our country money by cutting the White House staff by about 25 percent. Nothing personal; she would trim the fat, so to speak. It's difficult for Sherri to let other people help with the things that she feels she can do perfectly well for herself. She is a take-charge kind of woman. If something needs to be done, Sherri would go ahead and do it herself, rather than hiring someone else.

We could use more people like Sherri and Betty in Washington, don't you think?

By the way, did we mention they're fine?

IS THERE A DOCTOR
IN THE (WHITE) HOUSE?

A few presidential candidates are making national health care a priority in their campaign. Not us. We happen to disagree with a government-run national health care system. We agree that health care should be made available to all our citizens. We just don't happen to think that the government is the right entity to provide and oversee such a system.

Let's think about this for a moment. Historically, what departments have run more smoothly after being put under the government's oversight . . . ?

Exactly.

Let's take them one by one:

Social Security? That's worked out, hasn't it? All you've got to do is figure out how to live on $234 a month, and you've got it made.

Our postal system? Ever mail a letter across town and have it take the scenic route through Nova Scotia? We're not blaming the postal employees, just the government's involvement in the operation.

What about our bridges? Some bridges are collapsing right underneath us, and all anyone can do is point the finger to the "other guy." Call us picky, but when we have to drive our car across a bridge, we'd rather it not become a submarine.

The government seems to have no problem repairing our roads. In fact, they'll spend years repairing the same stretch of highway. Some sections have been under construction so long the "Road Work Ahead" signs are cemented in.

While we're on the subject of road repair, who decided that it would be a good idea to work on our highways at night? It used to be that you hardly ever had to worry about evening traffic. Now, they funnel you down to one lane and feed you by a construction site at three miles-per-hour. Month after month after month. Don't get us wrong. We're not saying the road workers are laying down on the job. They're not. Some of them can nap perfectly fine standing up.

We're not coming down on the road workers, necessarily. Both of us have had household projects that have taken years to finish up, too. But we've had to answer to a higher authority—our wives. There is no way we could rip out our driveway, set up lights on it every night, and then just stand there and shoot the breeze with our neighbors.

Betty and Sherri would make sure the project got finished in a timely manner. They would make sure that enough funds were set aside to finish the job. There would be no discussion on the matter. Period. (Come to think of it, if elected, perhaps we should appoint our wives to head up the National Transportation System. Our highways would be fixed within a reasonable amount of time—or else all construction workers would have to sleep on the couch.)

The point we're making is this: If our roads are still under construction years after the project was started, and if our bridges are crumbling under us, what makes us think that putting the government in charge of our health care would be a good idea?

If you took a survey, the overwhelming majority of the American people would probably say that they don't trust most politicians. Not that there aren't plenty of honest, hard-working politicians around who clearly have our best interest in mind. There are. But you've got to admit, the few bad apples have stunk up the basket pretty good. When the government gets involved in something, progress tends to get bogged down.

I (Bubba) don't know about you, but I don't want to find out that I've got five months to live, yet the soonest the government health care official can work me in for a visit with a specialist is in six months. That's one month too late. Do the math.

Nor do I want my doctor working with outdated technology (leeches come to mind) because he or she can't get government approval for more modern equipment.

If I am dying and desperately need a new heart, the last thing I want my surgeon's mind to be filled with is worries about when the government check will arrive. I want my surgeon to focus on the operation, and then, if he or she wants to go out and play another eighteen holes of golf, go for it . . . right after I'm all stitched up. If surgeons have money worries, they might be tempted to take on more surgeries than they have time for, and leave us to self-stitch our chest cavities! I don't want someone who is angry, broke, and planning a coup by night due to hatred of all the government regulations, performing heart transplants by day. I don't want to wait in my doctor's waiting room long enough to see Haley's comet come around again.

And I don't want to be limited to the medicines or hopelessness of yesterday. If I ever get that flesh-eating virus, I want to be able to do something other than say, "Bon appetit." If I get sick, I want the best medical care available, and I feel that I am the one best suited to find it. There is no way that the government is going to be more concerned about my health than I am.

Do you know our Constitution doesn't promise us health care? Where does it say that my neighbor is responsible to pay for my medical needs? Article 3? Article 4?

The answer is it doesn't.

Is health care too expensive? Sure, it is. But a national health care plan isn't the answer. Self-restraint in the medical community and among insurance companies is certainly part of the answer.

We've got a few other ideas to help. How about some medical discount coupons? If you need, say, an appendectomy, why can't they throw in a gall bladder removal for free? Or why can't they give out Frequent Patient cards, sort of like frequent flyer miles, where after you pay for your knee replacement surgery and your tonsillectomy, your third surgery is on the house?

With all of its problems, our medical system is still hard to beat. Not everyone will admit it, but isn't it interesting how some people in countries with socialized medicine, where they're waiting in long lines at clinics and praising how much better their system is than ours, will end up rushing to America for their own health care when they're about to die?

That's probably something we should note.

Again, we're not saying our medical system doesn't need overhauling. It absolutely does. Do we need to make health care affordable for every American? No question about it. Has the cost of medical care risen dramatically over the past decade? Anyone who's been to a doctor lately knows that.

We just don't happen to believe that getting the government involved is going to be the answer we're all looking for.

Part of the medical crisis in America is that too many of us go to the doctor for every little thing. Hypochondriacs are flooding the market and are responsible in part for medical prices skyrocketing. In most cases, acid reflux is not a permanent disability, entitling you to retire early and get disability payments from the government. Psoriasis shouldn't put you in a rest home for the remainder of your life. No matter how bad it is, halitosis does not require hospitalization. Just a good mouthwash.

It is for this reason that we, if elected, are going to start the "Suck it up, America" campaign. We want people to stop going to their doctor for things that could easily heal up on their own.

We've gotten soft, people. America used to turn out strong men and women who could weather almost anything. Abraham Lincoln used to split logs in the snow. The pioneers traveled West in covered wagons (without Aquafina water bottles, mind you). Do you think they complained about Restless Leg Syndrome?

We call what has happened to us "the Puddinization of America." We get a cold now and check ourselves into ICU. We make the doctor run a battery of tests, and then, if he or she can't find what's wrong with us, we run to another doctor and start all over again.

If we are elected co-presidents, we intend to change all that. With our "Suck it up, America" health care program, hospitalization will be *100 percent disallowed if it meets one or more of the following conditions:*

★ The "near fatal car wreck" you were just involved in was between you and a shopping cart.

★ You send for the MedEvac helicopter just because you're trying to keep the miles down on your Mercedes.

★ Your respiratory problems started after opening your monthly cell phone bill.

★ Your unexplained abdominal swelling followed a hot dog eating contest where you beat out Takeru Kobayashi.

★ That mysterious ringing in your ear can in any way be traced to the iPod wire hanging out of it.

★ Your heart palpitations cease once you make your final decision at Baskin Robbins.

★ The only broken bone in your x-ray is from the chicken leg you were eating during your MRI.

★ Your hangnail can be treated any other way.

★ Your feelings of disorientation and confusion followed the last presidential debate.

By simply implementing the above requirements, we figure we can cut the rate of unnecessary hospitalizations by half. And we would be well on our way to reforming medical care in this country.

Suck it up, America. It has quite a ring to it, doesn't it?

RICK AND BUBBA'S PATIENTS' BILL OF RIGHTS

Our nation has a citizens' bill of rights. Well, all citizens get sick at one time or another, don't they? And then what do they become? Patients! So, as logic demands, we now introduce our Patients' Bill of Rights.

1. *If your examination turns up nothing, your bill should be nothing.*

We don't know about you, but we're tired of sitting for an hour in a doctor's waiting room with our pack of children, and then another forty-five minutes in the examination room, only to be told in thirty seconds or less that what we thought was life-threatening is only a minor virus that will have to run its course. Then, without blinking they add, "Thank you. That will be one hundred seventy-five dollars." *For what?* Can't someone just check us out in the waiting room and save us all some time and money?

(And anyway, why should a hypochondriac have to pay real money for a fake illness? If the sickness is in his head, can't the payment be in his head, too?)

2. *Magazines must be no older than one month.*

I (Rick) was in a doctor's office the other day and was shocked to learn that Jimmy Carter had just been elected president.

If doctors are going to continue having outdated magazines, then they should be forced to charge the fees that coincide with the date on the magazine. In other words, if the magazine is from the 1970s, then the doctor's fee has to coincide with a typical doctor's fee from the 1970s. What was it back then? About ten bucks? And that included a lollipop.

3. *If a child patient is diagnosed with strep throat, parents have a right to refuse the ten days of bubble gum flavored oral antibiotic and instead order an injection of antibiotics.*

I (Rick) remember when I was young, the doctor would just give me a shot of penicillin and I'd be outside playing ball the next day. The needle was the size of a javelin, but it worked. Now, unless you're under the age of one, you hardly ever hear a doctor recommend a shot. Many of them will simply prescribe bubble gum flavored medicine, and after ten days, if it still hasn't worked, they'll switch it to cherry.

4. *A patient cannot be fooled into thinking she or he is about to see the doctor only to duped by the "We just need to weigh you, take your temperature, see how tall you are, and then we're going to send you back to the waiting room in shame" ploy.*

Why is it so hard to get in to see a doctor anyway? In some cases it's like trying to get past security to see a rock star. If you try to call him or her, you have to go through the receptionist who puts you through to a nurse practitioner, who will then ask you a few questions. If, after that, she deems it important enough, she will patch you through to the doctor's appointment desk where his booking secretary will give you the earliest available appointment (hopefully within the same decade, depending on his or her specialty).

And then, after waiting seven hours in a room filled with coughing, hacking people, your moment finally arrives and someone calls your name. With hope in your heart, you step briskly to see the person who will solve all your health woes . . . only to find you have just made it to Phase 2 of the waiting process—the examination room.

5. *If you are going to weigh us, do not ask what we weighed before. Just look at the scale, note the number in your head, and then write it down.*

Please do not make any comment, noise, or reference to any weight gain. This amounts to cruel and unusual punishment and should be the number one rule under the Right to Privacy Act. If the medical establishment is going to go to all the trouble they go to in order to keep our prescriptions and diagnosis private, they should at least be discreet about how much weight we've gained in the past year.

6. *A patient has the right to ask the doctor to not make the statement "Just relax," if he plans on checking his prostate.*

These are wasted words. (The same rule applies to the mammogram or that yearly exam for a woman.)

7. *The patient has the right to a more detailed explanation of the degree of pain that can be expected during any medical procedure.*

"You may experience some discomfort" or the classic "This may sting a little" is misleading. Do doctors take us for fools? The words, "This may sting a little" and the uncapping of a three-inch needle do not go together under any circumstances.

8. *Patients have the right to expect something a little more advanced to check our throat than being choked by a Popsicle stick.*

We're doing heart transplants these days, for goodness's sake. Why haven't we updated the throat exam? If doctors insist on using this archaic practice, then the least they could do is leave some of the Popsicle on it.

9. *If a patient is about to go under the knife for some surgical procedure, he or she should be allowed to wear something a little snappier than a bottomless hospital gown.*

Why are we still wearing these things? They may have been fine during the Depression, but times are better now. With what hospitals charge us per day for a typical hospital stay, couldn't they sew in a back on our gowns? Is that asking too much? Or better yet, why don't they give us gym shorts and a tank top?

10. *Edible treats for good behavior shall not be limited to child patients.*

It hardly seems fair, does it? The kid's getting stuck one time with a needle, while the parents who are holding him or her down can get kicked multiple times by Junior's flailing arms and legs. Parents have also been known to have their hands squeezed so tightly it stops all blood flow to that extremity for a week. Then, when handed the bill, parents have to give up a week's salary to pay for all that pain and suffering. If kids get lollipops and glow-in-the-dark stickers for taking one measly shot, shouldn't their parents at least get a chocolate bar for having to hold them down?

In fact, we think there should be an Adult's Treat Chart posted at every doctor's office and medical center in the country. Here are our suggestions of what should be on it:

★ Rick and Bubba's Medical Procedure Treat Chart for Adults ★

Gall stone:	Homemade apple pie
Tonsillitis:	Not just ice cream. We're thinking banana split.
Treadmill:	Milkshake
Blood work:	Pick your own pasta dish.
MRI:	Chinese, probably sesame chicken
Slipped disc:	Dinner at a meat-and-three
Prostate exam:	All-expense-paid hunting trip for at least three days
Mammogram:	Flowers and Godiva truffles
Lower GI (with enema):	All-expense-paid trip to anywhere Southwest flies
Colonoscopy:	A certified psychological counselor at no charge—and some time alone . . .

OUR CABINET

One of the nice things about being president is that you get to pick your own cabinet. We have both installed cabinets in our homes before, so we feel prepared for this job and have given serious thought as to who we would want to place in these key positions of power. It can't be just anybody. It has to be people we can trust, people who will have our backs, and people who we are in some way indebted to. Let's be honest, a cabinet position can be a major payback. A president can pay off all sorts of personal favors by handing out cabinet positions.

We've given a lot of thought as to who we would like to serve in our cabinet. Naturally, we would include the members of our radio staff: Speedy, Don Juan, Ryan Greenwood, Greg Burgess, and all the others. But for the official positions, the ones that require a little more political experience, we have had to reach outside the Rick and Bubba family.

The following is our dream cabinet, in part:

Treasury Secretary: Dave Ramsey of Financial Peace University and radio personality. Dave "I'm better than I deserve" Ramsey is the perfect person to oversee our national budget. Dave will have the nation out of debt by the end of our first term. We might lose the presidential limo out of the deal and have to drive around in a paid-off Hyundai, but our deficit will be a thing of the past if Dave has anything to say about it.

Department of the Interior: Martha Stewart. She's perfect. And after her incarceration, she should have plenty to talk about with some of the other Washington political figures.

Department of Energy: Rick's brother, Greg Burgess. If the Kennedy clan can hire each other, why not the Burgess bunch? Greg is a pole climber for the Alabama Power Company. He knows about energy.

Secretary of Health and Human Services: Betty Lou Bussey. Betty is a registered nurse. We won't make her Surgeon General (because of certain incidents we shall describe later), but she is more than qualified to serve on the cabinet in this capacity. And she's thorough. Before I (Bubba) met Betty, I never knew there were so many places where you could check someone's pulse. You know what they say, once you marry a nurse, you'll never go back.

Secretary of Veteran Affairs: Ollie North. Nobody cares more for the men and women who put on our military uniform every day than Ollie North. He bleeds veteran. He wins this post hands down.

Department of Transportation: Dale Earnhardt Jr. Hey, this is obvious. Who knows more about transportation than Dale Earnhardt? He turns five hundred every weekend. With Dale, 55 mph speed limits would be a thing of the past.

Head of the Federal Drug Administration: Clark Howard from WSB radio in Atlanta. As a well-experienced consumer advocate, Clark Howard will look out for the public's welfare like no other FDA official in history.

Secretary of Defense: Sean Hannity. There is nobody better to have on your side in a fight than someone with conservative values and a New York City taxi driver mentality. What foreign country wouldn't be afraid of that?

Secretary of State: Speedy. He is always looking for a way to work problems out peacefully. He is a true diplomat who never lets the red hair that he used to have get in the way. We can easily picture him sitting around a table with everyone in the Middle East and working out some sort of compromise. Or at least having some good laughs. (And wouldn't it be great if he were able to negotiate some Speedy Treaties?)

Secretary of Education: Gene Rhodes, my (Bubba) eighth grade grammar school teacher and to this day a good friend. I can't think of a man who's more passionate about education than Gene Rhodes. I also promised him that if I ever got to a place where I could pay him back for some of the encouragement he gave me, I'd give him a job. If I'm elected president, I'd live up to my word. But friendship aside, Gene would be great in that position. He takes such an aggressive approach to education that people would be screaming "Bring back the 'No child left behind' days! We need a break!" Gene has the charisma, knowledge, and political skills to make the office of the Department of Education great again. If he survived our eighth grade class, he can survive Washington.

Secretary of Agriculture: Garry Vines. Who is Garry Vines? He's the hunting camp bulldozer guy. Every hunting camp has to have a Garry Vines bulldozer guy. He does all the work we need done at the hunting camp. He cleans the underbrush, keeps the roads clear. He is Mr. Outdoors, Mr. Agriculture. He is so talented, he could build a cruise missile out of a vacuum cleaner. There is no job out in the woods that Garry couldn't do.

Chief of Staff: Rush Limbaugh. Rush Limbaugh isn't afraid to tell it like it is, and he's funny, too. We think he would make a great Chief of Staff. Besides, he's a radio man, and we radio guys have to stick together.

Head of the Internal Revenue Service: Willie Nelson. This is really a no brainer. Why in the world would we put an accountant in this position? We need someone there who has been on the other side of the auditor's desk and felt the pain. Willie wins this position hands down.

Top Five Candidates for Vice President

1. **Mother Teresa.** There's not a single skeleton in her closet. The fact that she's no longer with us shouldn't matter because you don't usually hear that much from the vice president anyway.

2. **Tom Hanks.** He survived being a castaway with only a soccer ball to talk to. He's perfect for VP.

3. **Mike Huckabee.** We love his sense of humor, but the diet has to go.

4. **Regis Philbin.** That's the only thing he hasn't yet done.

5. **No one.** Would anyone really even notice?

FIRST KIDS

When I look at what my kids have done to my own house, I can't imagine what they will do to 1600 Pennsylvania Avenue if ever given the chance. You think the Bush twins were in the news a lot? Just wait until the Rick Burgess offspring get to Washington. They'll be riding their skateboards up and down the halls, playing in the White House elevator, and drawing mustaches on all the portraits. And that's just while they're in time-out.

But don't let that stop any of you from voting for us. It's not like the White House is full of irreplaceable heirlooms. . . . All right, maybe I should rephrase that. All I'm saying is, when a foreign dignitary stops by the White House to visit, don't you think it will be a lot more fun for them to be greeted by a bunch of kids riding four wheelers across the lawn, than just a group of photographers competing for the best posed photo op?

Honestly, the biggest problem we can see is when we can't find a babysitter and our kids have to go along with us to address Congress. The speaker of the house and our vice president will be seated directly behind us, and climbing all over their laps will be the Killer Bs, dressed as Spiderman, all making goofy faces at the camera. We could probably get the vice president and the speaker to stop, but there's not telling how long the Killer Bs will do it.

Rowdy presidential offspring are nothing new to Washington. Historians tell us that some of the children of our former presidents misbehaved quite often while their dads were busy at work in the Oval Office. Abraham Lincoln's son Tad once brought a pair of goats into the White House and harnessed them to a kitchen chair. (Apparently, he liked his milk fresh.) The goats then dragged the chair through the East Room, where a group of Bostonian women were meeting. The women had to dive out of the way to avoid getting rammed by the goats. You know they had to have taken up the matter with Poor Abe later, as if the man wasn't depressed enough already.

Then, there were Theodore Roosevelt's offspring. Teddy and his wife had six children living at the White House, ranging in age from three to sixteen. And then there were the family animals. The Roosevelts (who didn't agree with our No Pets in the White House philosophy) had cats, dogs, raccoons, snakes, badgers, a macaw, and even a pony.

One story that has been passed down through the years is that once when Archie Roosevelt was bedridden, his brothers snuck his pony into the White House, leading the animal down the hall and even putting him on the White House elevator!

Yeah, I could see my kids doing something like that.

John Kennedy's kids also acted up a bit while residing at 1600 Pennsylvania Avenue. John Jr. used to sneak into the Oval Office and hide under his daddy's desk. There's no telling how many government secrets the boy overheard.

With one hundred thirty-two rooms in the White House, I could see my kids having a hide-and-seek marathon. Who knows? Once we moved to the White House, we might go months without seeing our kids.

Under the Clinton presidency, it wasn't so much their daughter, but rather some high-powered friends of theirs who turned the Lincoln bed into a trampoline. Bubba and I would never do such a thing. First of all, we would go through the mattress on the first jump. Second, our national treasures were not made for practicing cannonballs on. We're talking about the bed that President Abraham Lincoln slept in. You don't jump on the bed Lincoln slept in.

Even though a precedent for rambunctious children at the White House has already been set, we pledge to you, the American public, that if elected co-presidents, we will do everything in our power to make sure our kids stay in line.

Of course, we make that same pledge to their teachers every year, and well, let's just say the school keeps us on speed dial.

CAMPAIGN SLOGANS

Campaign slogans are important to a presidential race. In the commercial world, a good product advertisement can increase sales, and in the political world, a clever slogan can increase votes.

Over the years, presidential candidates, or their handlers, have come up with some interesting slogans.

How inspiring was William McKinley's 1900 reelection campaign slogan, "Let Well Enough Alone"? That makes you want to rush out and vote for the guy, doesn't it?

Barry Goldwater's 1964 campaign slogan was another doozy: "In Your Heart You Know He's Right." That only opened the door for some of his opponents' parody slogan, "In Your Guts You Know He's Nuts."

Campaign slogans, good or bad, play a vital role in a presidential campaign. That's why we've given a lot of thought to our campaign slogan, and have narrowed it down to the following top ten:

Top Ten Rick and Bubba Campaign Slogans

We've elected clowns before. Let's try comedians.

Vote for Rick and Bubba—Things Couldn't Get Any Worse

Rick and Bubba—Two Presidents We'll Never Have to Watch Jog

The Buck Stops Here. But We'll Accept Checks.

Rick and Bubba for Co-Presidents—A Side of Beef in Every Pot!

Rick and Bubba—No Meal Left Behind

Rick and Bubba—Bringing Barbequed Wings to the West Wing

Send Rick and Bubba to Washington—What Else Do They Have to Do?

Rick and Bubba—Hey, They're Available

Elect Rick and Bubba—Let the World Question the Mental Stability of Our Leaders for a Change

(That last one's a little long but it still has a nice ring to it, don't you think?)

WHY BETTY WILL NOT BE SURGEON GENERAL

Rick and I both love Betty. She has been a wonderful wife to me, and a great supporter of both Rick and me. On the surface, you would think that with her nursing credentials we would have listed her as the logical choice for Surgeon General. But by Betty's own admission, she might not be the right person for the position. There are some incidents that have occurred while she was doing home health care that might come to light and cause the nation some concern. Nothing too serious, just . . . well, I suppose in the spirit of full disclosure I should just come right out with it: There were times when Betty showed up at the wrong house.

"When I was doing home health," Betty said while being interviewed for the position, "I would go to a patient's home, do the exam, fill out the paperwork, call the doctor to give my report, and then suddenly realize that I was supposed to be visiting the person next door."

We are not proud of this revelation, and we're quite sure it was nothing more than an innocent oversight. Still, we want to be forthright. Apparently, there were several, no, more than several, there were four or five . . . okay, we can't really tell you how many times Betty would come home from a day of home nursing and say, "Well, I did an exam on someone, but it was the wrong person."

When you are interviewing candidates to be surgeon general, "I did an exam on someone, but it was the wrong person" are not words you want to hear.

I finally had to ask her one day, "Why don't the people stop you, Betty? I can't believe they let you walk in and just start examining them?"

Betty shrugged and said, "They're often elderly, and I guess they're thrilled that someone's at their door, whoever it is. They'll see me standing there and say, 'Come on in, honey, let's talk.'"

"But at what point in the examination do you realize you're at the wrong house?" I asked.

"When I'm writing notes down in their chart and things aren't matching up. Or it's after I call the doctor and he asks how high her blood pressure is, and I have to say '*her*'? Thank goodness I usually notice the error before the patient has any blood work done. Or outpatient surgical procedures."

Again, we're only sharing this information in the interest of full disclosure. It is not intended to cause Betty, any of her patients, or for that matter their neighbors, any embarrassment.

Can you imagine the scene after one of Betty's unintended medical exams?

As soon as she realizes the error, apologizes to the eighty-year-old man she just examined, and leaves, he probably calls up his old army buddy and says, *"Hey, Bernie. You're not gonna believe this! You know that fantasy I've always had about answering the front door and a beautiful blonde is standing there? Well, it just happened. I'm telling ya, she appeared out of nowhere and said she was here for my examination. I didn't even know I was sick, but I can tell you, I'm sure feeling a lot better now!"*

It doesn't only happen with Betty's patients either. Once, when we were house shopping, Betty drove up to a home and immediately fell in love with the property. Figuring she'd check out the backyard first, she went ahead and let our kids start playing on the yard equipment. The house had an outdoor fireplace, a nice pool area; it was beautiful. We loved it and started to make our way inside when the owner of the house ran out and asked what in the world we were doing in her backyard playing on her swing set?

"We're looking at your house," Betty explained.

"Well, it's not for sale!" the woman said.

Betty had the wrong address again. In Betty's defense, though, she had thought it was a new listing and that they just didn't have the sign up yet. But Betty didn't let the mistake deter her. Since our kids seemed to be getting along so well with the homeowner's little girl, Betty exchanged names and phone numbers, and all the kids became playmates.

As much as we love Betty, it's probably best that she not be considered for the surgeon general position, and definitely not for secretary of state either. If we ever have to fight in Iran, she'll have us showing up in India.

THE HEAT'S ON

Let us make one thing perfectly clear. We are not sure we believe all these environmental warnings from the so-called experts about global warming. The earth may indeed be getting warmer, but who's to say that it isn't due to something else—like all the baby boomers hitting middle age at the same time and cranking up their thermostats?

Even if global warming is for real, even if there is a hole in the ozone layer the size of Minnesota, we believe our best scientific minds will eventually come up with something that will fix the problem. After all, weren't these the same people who invented Velcro?

Without getting into the whole global warming controversy, we can't help but wonder if some people aren't milking the issue for what they can personally get out of it. Y2K comes to mind. What if someone somewhere out there is making a fortune using fear tactics, and all of us are naively buying into it?

Think about it—if you've stayed in a hotel recently, you've no doubt read the signs in your room asking you to help the hotel save water. The management wants you to reuse your towels and sleep in the same sheets in order to join with them in saving Planet Earth. But have you ever thought they could really just be wanting us to help them save Planet Water Bill?

If we let the hotels off the hook on this one, other companies might start asking us to give them a pass on some of their services and blame it on the environment, too. Before long we could be reading signs like:

"Due to the gas crisis, our taxis will now only be taking you halfway to your destination. If you will do your part and get out and walk the rest of the way, we will be saving our resources for future generations. You will, of course, still be charged the full cab fare, and your driver will continue to take the longest route to your destination. We trust you understand. Thank you for your cooperation."

Or how about this one:

"Due to the growing obesity problem in America (no pun intended), we will now begin monitoring your plate at our all-you-can-eat buffet. We realize we began as an all-you-can-eat enterprise, but we didn't realize how much you people could eat. You have been cutting into our profits, uh, we mean, not taking care of your health, and we want to do our part to be responsible citizens and help you maintain a healthy lifestyle. Any plate piled so high it does not meet the ceiling fan clearance will be immediately confiscated and returned to the serving trays."

Or:

"As a result of the news report stating that cell phone usage could be linked to brain tumors, we will now be charging a $200 per month tumor risk surcharge. Our reasoning behind this? We have none. We are the phone company and do not now nor ever need to explain ourselves."

If you think it would end there, it wouldn't. The following notices may also be in our future:

"Because of our greed in getting unqualified borrowers into sub-prime mortgages that they could not possibly afford, and because of the greed of those who bought million-dollar houses or half-million dollar condos with an adjustable

interest rate and their payments have now doubled, and in some instances even tripled, in recent months, and because we're pretty sure the government will come to our aid and bail us out so we won't lose the fortunes we made off these loans, we will now be raising our lending standards. Only those who do not need to borrow will now qualify to borrow money. This is for the good of the country, maintaining our own net worth, and we're pretty sure it can also be directly linked to improving global warming."

"In consideration of the environment, we will no longer be serving complimentary water to our dining guests. We will, however, be offering lobster that has been boiled in a tub of water (available to you at $36 a serving), soup that contains large quantities of water (available to you at $8 per bowl), and of course, bottled water (available to you at $4 a bottle). Thank you for passing on your 6-ounce serving of free water and helping us save our planet."

"Due to global warming, we are forced to increase our medical fees yet again. Our annual physician's fishing trip to Alaska has been hampered due to the melting ice caps, and we have no other choice than to pass the expense of finding another vacation spot at this late date along to our patients. Also, the thirty-five-dollars-per-dose aspirin we have been charging has been doubled to cover the cost for our rechargeable light bulbs. Thank you for your understanding in this matter."

As you can see, global warming may turn out to be one of the biggest scams in the history of the world. Or maybe not. At this point, who (besides Al Gore) really knows for sure?

It doesn't seem feasible, though, that hairspray could be the culprit for global warming. If that were the case, wouldn't it have happened back in the 1950s and 1960s when we were all using a lot more of it? One beehive alone could've been responsible for all the damage to the ozone layer.

Have you heard the latest theory? They're now looking into the idea that global warming might be the result of years of "emissions" from all the cows and moose on our planet. Can they really tell us that with a straight face? They can and they are. But once they start blaming global warming on cows and moose burping and breaking wind, the whole credibility of this issue starts going down the tubes. (And how are we supposed to help conserve cow belches anyway?)

Do you remember back in 1974 when an article in *Time* magazine claimed that we were heading toward another ice age and that we were all going to freeze? Temperatures on earth were getting cooler, and apparently had been for the previous three decades. Supposedly, it was just a matter of time before the whole earth would look like a giant snow cone.

So what happened? Our parkas and mukluks are still hanging by our front doors, but so far we haven't needed them here in Birmingham. How's it going for the rest of you? Did any of you notice an Ice Age? A glacier in your driveway is a little hard to miss.

The truth is the predicted Ice Age never showed up. They scared us with that back then and now it's global warming. Ice age. Global warming. Ice age. Global warming. It sounds like a husband and wife fighting over the blankets.

Maybe the earth is just naturally going through cycles. Maybe it heats up and cools down all by itself. The warmest years on record weren't last year or the year before that or the year before that. They weren't even in the last decade. They were between 1930 and 1934.

We also think the global warming people would look a lot more credible if they'd show up at their speaking engagements riding a bicycle, instead of in their gas guzzling private jets or stretched limousines.

And have you heard about these new "carbon offsets"? The theory is that if you can't stop committing crimes against Mother Earth by driving a SUV or using plastic grocery bags, then you can go to a certain Web site and purchase carbon offsets. When you've saved enough of them, they will plant a tree somewhere in the world to balance out your guilt. Kind of like modern-day "indulgences," except without a Catholic priest. (We really think the whole concept of carbon offsets came about so that some celebrities can feel better about the airplane runway they are operating in their backyards.)

If these offsets catch on, we're thinking about coming out with "fat offsets." Every time you feel guilty about going through a drive-thru, you can send us a hundred dollars, and we'll eat a stalk of celery for you. And maybe a burger.

As co-presidents, we want to focus on environmental concerns that are happening now, not ones predicted to happen in the future. There are plenty of concerns right now, and we should be doing everything in our power to fix them. For one example, we don't want to catch a fish with so much mercury it could show us the temperature of the water.

The bottom line is this—America is blessed. We're so blessed that sometimes it seems we look around for reasons to feel guilty. Why can't we just enjoy the natural cycles of the earth and admit that when God created our universe, He knew exactly what He was doing? And anyway, even if the whole earth really is heating up, it has quite a ways to go before catching up to an Alabama summer.

RICK AND BUBBA'S BACKWARD PLAN FOR AMERICA

The following are some talking points for one of our future radio addresses (for full effect, read to the tune of patriotic music):

America needs to get back to a time when being "neighborly" had nothing to do with what you see on *Desperate Housewives*.

America needs to get back to a time when the family dinner table didn't include a drive-thru.

America needs to get back to a time when respect was more than a Golden Oldies song.

America needs to get back to a time when parents spent more time with their kids and less time with their cell phones.

America needs to get back to a time when we were more embarrassed to swear in public than we were to pray in public.

America needs to get back to a time when parents saved for family vacations instead of implants and tummy tucks.

America needs to get back to a time when the only thing a student had to fear at school was the cafeteria food.

America needs to get back to a time when we cared more about people than an endangered gnat.

America needs to get back to a time when you got in more trouble for using profanity than for saying "Merry Christmas."

ONE NATION
UNDER GOD

It's hard to look at America's history and not see the evidence of God's blessing on this country. We don't always deserve it. We've taken Him out of our schools, and some have even tried to take Him out of our pledge of allegiance, but He still keeps blessing us.

We're not ashamed to say that we pray to God for His guidance in our lives, we pray for our leaders, and we even pray for our enemies (although on September 11, 2001, that wasn't an easy thing to do).

Prayer is good. It's what got both of us our diplomas. It's what gets us through traffic jams, credit card disputes, and parent-teacher conferences.

What would our founding fathers have to say about how we're treating the subject of separation of church and state? Maybe they already gave us their two-cents worth:

"God governs in the affairs of man; and if a sparrow cannot fall to the ground without His notice, is it probable that an empire can rise without His aid?"

—Benjamin Franklin

"We've staked the future of all our political institutions upon our capacity . . . to sustain ourselves according to the Ten Commandments of God."

—James Madison

"The Almighty hath implanted in us these inextinguishable feelings for good and wise purposes. They are the guardians of His image in our heart. They distinguish us from the herd of common animals."

—Thomas Paine

"If thou wouldst rule well, thou must rule for God, and to do that, thou must be ruled by Him. . . . Those who will not be governed by God will be ruled by tyrants."

—William Penn

Somewhere along the line we got the misconception that the government was supposed to protect us *from* religion instead of guaranteeing us our freedom *of* religion. Funny how misunderstanding one little preposition can do so much damage!

Just like our forefathers, faith will be an important part of our administration. We will not rename the White House Christmas tree the White House Holiday Decorated Botanical Display. Prayer will be put back in school (at least until our kids get their diplomas). And "In God We Trust" will continue to be printed on our money (it's been a while since we've held onto any money long enough to inspect it, but we're pretty sure that phrase is still on there).

Faith is an important layer of our nation's foundation, and we believe it is God's blessing that has held this country together. But some things have certainly changed over the years. Twenty-five years ago, at my (Rick) high school in Oxford, Alabama (Oxford is the bathroom stop between Birmingham and Atlanta), students would drive their trucks into that school parking lot every day, with rifles and shotguns up on the dash. I would say that probably 30 percent of the cars had hunting rifles in them.

You know what? There wasn't a single shot ever fired at our school. Why? I believe it was because we had a healthy respect for and fear of God. We also had a respect for and fear of our dads. My father could set a shotgun on the table and tell us not to touch it, and we wouldn't touch it. It was that simple. We knew right from wrong.

Today, we debate things like what the word *"is"* really means, or whether or not a homeowner is liable for the medical expenses of a burglar who suffers a heart attack because the homeowner came home early and startled him. It's crazy! As co-presidents, we will put an end to insane litigation like this and return some sanity to our lives.

Well, at least as much sanity as either one of us can spare.

SETTING A FEW
THINGS STRAIGHT

After we win the election, one of the first pictures in the news will be of moving vans in front of the United Nations building. We've never really understood the United Nations. It meets here on our soil, but it doesn't seem to pay us very much respect. It's like an out-of-town guest who complains about everything from the cooking to what's on TV. Sooner or later you find yourself wanting to say, "Sorry you have to leave. Here's your hat and coat."

After seeing some of their actions over the last few years, we'd like to give the United Nations its hat and coat. The lack of respect has a lot to do with it, but it's mainly because we don't want to see our troops fighting in baby blue helmets. Who came up with the idea of baby blue helmets anyway? That could be why the United Nations' mandates don't have more muscle. It's those helmets. No one takes baby blue helmets seriously.

While we're at it, we would also make it a crime for the French to say anything negative about America. If it wasn't for us, they'd all be speaking German right now.

Are you getting the message that these presidential co-candidates are a little tired of being pushed around by the rest of the world? America is a super power, and while we usually don't mind being called upon to help out our friends, and we will continue to use tremendous restraint in the face of our enemies, we believe it's time America explained a few basic ground rules to everyone:

#1 If you try to take over the world, we will shut you down. Sorry, but this is your only option. It's our world, too, and we take our freedoms seriously. (As a side note to all you tyrannical dictators, how about spending less money on missiles to take over the world, and more money on food for your citizens? Just a thought.)

#2 Do not call on us to fight a war for you if you have not paid us for your last one.

#3 Do not expect us to have your back in a war if you cannot have our back at a press conference.

#4 We like to win wars. If you ask us to come, kindly allow us do that. Our military are not social workers. They do not want to solve all your problems or run your country. Their job is to win wars and defeat enemies of freedom. Let us do that, and then let us go home.

#5 We would rather not wear baby blue helmets.

#6 If you ask us to help you fight your war, please remember this later when someone asks you why we're in your country.

#7 If it's your war, we expect you to be fighting it along with us. No excuses.

#8 No matter what you may see on the news about your war, Americans will always stand behind our soldiers and honor their sacrifice. Please do the same.

#9 When we win your war, please get the story straight in your history books.

#10 When your country is free again, a simple thank-you would be appreciated. Better yet, when we have major disasters in our country, such as hurricanes, floods, tornadoes, or terrorist attacks, how about sending some help to us? We can't make you, of course, but it sure would be nice.

WASHINGTON MISHAPS

Remember when Vice President Dick Cheney accidentally shot his hunting partner? Or when former president Ronald Reagan got thrown from his horse? And how about when Gerald Ford's golf ball hit that spectator, or the time he tripped and fell off an airplane ramp in the rain in Salzburg? Or when Bob Dole took an accidental dive off the stage while campaigning for president?

See, that's proof positive—we *are* Washington material. We can do all of that and more. In fact, we've already got a story that might even beat those.

It was one of those trips that had *Survivor* written all over it. We were in Cabo San Lucas, and someone in our group (we forget who, but God recorded it) suggested we go snorkeling. It sounded like a good idea at the time. So did the Titanic.

Actually, it was a pretty good idea; it just wasn't the right day. Most people don't go snorkeling in the middle of a hurricane advisory. But then, we aren't most people. We are "politician material." *(Disclaimer: A lot of politicians are bright, forward-thinking individuals, dedicated to serving the American public. They just don't make the news very often.)*

We had been out in the boat about thirty minutes when the hurricane advisory for Cabo San Lucas came over the radio. I recall that it said something to the effect of "Death to all snorkelers!"

Since I was in the water about two feet from the boat, my initial instinct was to climb back into the vessel so I could be in a position to save the others. This is a survival tactic that I learned from Rick—always save yourself first so you can help out everyone else. What good can you do anybody if you're injured or killed? As much as I hate to brag on myself, I did manage to find the inner strength to save myself first. But then I noticed Rick struggling out in the water and realized in that one moment that if anything were to happen to him, I would have all those Rick and Bubba T-shirts to cross out his name on. I knew I had to do whatever it took to save him and as many of the others as I could.

The first thing I had to do was keep everyone calm so I could help them back into the boat. So I screamed, "Hurricane warning! Hurricane warning!" For some reason, pandemonium soon broke out. (Obviously, they couldn't handle the truth.)

As each one swam toward the boat, I did my best to help them to safety and comfort them by singing "Nearer My God to Thee." All of a sudden, one member of our party declared that he couldn't take it anymore. (I'm not sure if it was the turbulence of the waves or my singing.) The next thing I knew he had taken off and was swimming to shore.

I wanted to swim to shore myself, but my honor wouldn't let me leave the boat. That, and the fact that all of the food was still on the boat.

The storm grew worse. A huge wave hit our boat, and then another, and another. You could see the look of fear in everyone's eyes. The storm was growing in intensity. Would our captain be able to navigate his way back to shore, dodging the rocky cliffs that ran along the coastline? Only time would tell.

Have you ever noticed that in times like this, humor always seems to help? Rick and I started singing the theme to *Gilligan's Island*. It did seem to take everyone's mind off the gravity of our situation . . . and onto wanting to toss us overboard instead.

Rick and I were in the very back of the boat because someone thought it was best to put all the weight back there. But the ocean was too big and angry to outsmart. It was now pouring water into our boat faster than we could bail it out. We were fighting a losing battle. You know those scenes in old sea movies where the hero is fighting a huge sea monster, just as a monsoon is hitting? This was similar to one of those scenes.

Conditions were deteriorating right before our eyes. Rick looked up once and thought he saw Moby Dick.

Now any time I'm in grave danger, my mind starts visualizing how the story will be featured on CNN:

"Rick Burgess and Bill 'Bubba' Bussey, two radio personalities from Alabama, nearly drowned today while snorkeling during a hurricane advisory. Their seemingly lifeless bodies washed up on shore, but authorities didn't send for an ambulance for over fourteen hours. It wasn't until marine biologists ruled out the possibility of there being a couple of beached humpback whales that proper medical care finally arrived for the two unfortunate snorkelers."

My mind snapped back to reality. The waves were so high now, they looked like a wall of water all around us. The captain managed to get the boat turned around, and miraculously, we were now heading toward shore. Rick was bailing water as fast as he could, and the radio was still broadcasting its hurricane warnings "to any idiots who are still out on the water." It felt like a Griswold vacation movie and *Titanic* all rolled into one.

The waves were raging so violently that we couldn't even walk on the boat. We were being knocked down the minute we tried to stand up.

Although we were headed toward shore, progress was painfully slow against the monstrous storm. In a panic, everybody started jumping into the water in a "Hail Mary, we're going for it!" play.

And that, dear friends, is when it happened . . .

Right in the middle of all that chaos, all that rain, all that wind, Memaw, an eighty-year-old Mexican grandmother in a string bikini (that alone should have been a warning to us that the trip was doomed), got hit by one of the most vicious waves of the day. The wave came crashing down on her and, well, there's just no delicate way to put this—the wave left Memaw, but took her string bikini with it. When the water cleared, eighty-year-old Memaw was standing there, holding onto a rope for dear life without a stitch of clothes on!

Now, everyone who could swim at all jumped off the boat!

When I dove into the water, I laid out like the San Diego chicken. Rick jumped in next, and witnesses tell us that we both made it to shore in record time.

As for Memaw, we understand she eventually made it to shore, too. But her swimsuit has never been found. It's probably still floating somewhere in the Sea of Cortez.

All that to say if elected, we can handle *anything*.

WE DO
SOLEMNLY SWEAR

George Washington took his first oath of office on the balcony of Federal Hall in New York City. John Adams took his in the House of Representatives Chamber in Congress Hall in Philadelphia. James Monroe was sworn in just outside the Old Brick Capitol, which is now the site of the Supreme Court Building.

Our inauguration is going to be equally as impressive and symbolic. It will be held in front of the Big Boy statue, which we will move to Washington and place at the top of the steps on the west front of the Capitol Building for the ceremony. What other statue could we stand in front of at our oath-taking that would have a deeper meaning to the team of Rick and Bubba than the Big Boy statue?

This would by no means minimize the sincerity of the swearing-in ceremony. We know it is one of the most solemn occasions in our country. Every four years, another man (or woman), is chosen by the electorate to lead our great country. If we are lucky enough to be elected America's co-presidents, we will not take this day lightly.

One of the most important parts of Inauguration Day is the Oath of Office. For those of you who don't think a man should ever cry in public, we are giving you fair warning—we will tear up at the swearing-in ceremony. We tear up when placing our order at Long John Silver's. How could we not tear up at the Inauguration? When we place our hands on the Bible and take that oath of office that says "We solemnly swear that we will support and defend the Constitution of the United States against all enemies, foreign and domestic; that we will bear true faith and allegiance to the same; that we take this obligation freely, without any mental reservation or purpose of evasion; and that we will well and faithfully discharge the duties of the office on which we are about to enter . . . so help us God," there is no way to make it through that moment and not choke up. Throughout history, the victor of each hard-fought presidential race had to have choked up at some point during his oath. Maybe he hid it well, trying to look presidential and all, but there is no way the ceremony would not move you.

There also has to be a moment when the new president looks over at the incumbent president, a man he may have raked over the coals during the campaign, and he has to see him in a brand-new light. Suddenly, the outgoing president's advice seems pretty valuable. He wants to ask him about four thousand questions. And keep his cell phone number on speed dial.

Former presidents have been known to give some pretty good advice when leaving office. Like when outgoing president Ronald Reagan left a note for incoming president George H. W. Bush that had the heading, "Don't let the turkeys get you down."

If we're elected, we hope we get some good advice like that.

The whole ceremony has to be humbling, too. You're taking over the reins and it will now be your responsibility to lead the greatest nation on the face of the earth. No matter how excited you were on election night, on Inauguration Day it's a whole different feeling. We're pretty sure you mostly feel a great sense of humility as you pray for God's guidance for the next four years.

After the swearing-in ceremony, we will do what other presidents have done and lead a parade back to the White House. We love parades. We have been the Grand Marshals of numerous parades here in Alabama. We are experienced float sitters. (We once thought about getting a job where that's all you do. The title of "Professional Float Sitter" sounded good to us. We don't know what the pay is for something like that, but there can't be a lot of training involved. If you've got good balance and can get the wave down, you're pretty well set.)

We might even walk the parade route instead. It's not a very long walk; and besides, we hear there are some good hot dog vendors along the way.

After the ceremony and the parade, it'll be time to party! Since we have already said that even if we are elected to a second term, we will not be having a second inauguration, we would want to make sure we did it right the first time. But we wouldn't go overboard like some presidents have done in the past.

First of all, we will only have one party location. We don't see the need for multiple Inaugural Balls taking place all over town. We don't want to be arriving late at four or five other parties. By then, all the refreshments will be gone and people will be tired of waiting for us to show up. Let us just go to one party and stay there throughout the night.

As far as entertainment goes, we'll tell you now that we won't be booking Barbra Streisand. Not that we don't like her music. We do. Not because we don't like her politics, either. We don't agree with her on a lot of issues, but this is America and she's free to have her opinion, so that's not the reason either.

Since it's our inauguration, we feel it would be more fitting to use a group that can relate to the average American. A group like, well, like our own band, Mr. Lucky. Our band could use the national exposure, and best of all, we're free. We might even be setting a precedent. Has any president ever performed at his own Inaugural Ball? We're pretty sure Bill Clinton left his saxophone at home for both of his inaugurations. It was probably for the best.

The country might enjoy seeing their newly elected co-presidents singing and playing at the Inaugural Ball. They might even respect the fact that we're trying to save the country a little money. (The Rick and Bubba product table in the back of the room would be there only to get everyone's e-mail address to keep them informed of national matters . . . and of course, Mr. Lucky's tour dates. We wouldn't think of selling our products at an Inaugural Ball. That's what order forms are for.)

Then, when all the celebrating is over, the crowds have left, and the caterers are shooing us and our doggie bags away from the serving tables, we will gently take our wives in our arms, look into their eyes, and say the words that every president has no doubt said to his wife at the end of their own Inauguration Day . . .

"Honey, what in the world have I gotten us into? Dear God, help us!"

THE DEBATES

Last chapter we dreamed a little. We already had us at the Inaugural Ball. Now we will get back to the gritty reality: the presidential debates. We all know that the presidential debates are one of the best ways for voters to get an unfiltered look at the heart and convictions (and stage makeup) of the candidates. The candidates' sound bites won't give you the complete picture. Their bumper stickers are too pithy. You certainly can't get a fair impression of a candidate from the things his or her opponents are saying either.

But in a debate, you're not getting any spin. You're not getting some reporter's interpretation, and no one's putting words in a candidate's mouth. (Or at least the candidate has to recall whatever words somebody else put in his or her mouth.)

It's just the candidates answering the questions as honestly as they can.

We look forward to participating in the presidential debates. We haven't been invited yet, but since we've recently moved our radio studio, we figure the invitation might have gotten lost in the mail.

So we are going ahead and preparing for the debates anyway, and we'll just show up. Since we have a lot of our own studio equipment, we can even bring our own microphones in case they don't have enough.

We won't know until that night what questions will be asked. No candidate does. But we have gone ahead and written out a few mock questions to help us prepare. We're including them here just for fun. If any of these questions happen to get asked in one of the real debates, try not to look like you already know our answer.

QUESTION: So, why a co-presidency?

ANSWER: Neither one of us wanted to be vice-president.

QUESTION: How might your lives change if you are elected as co-presidents of the United States?

ANSWER: With a presidential motorcade, it'll take longer to go through the drive-thru.

QUESTION: Being political outsiders, what would you both be bringing to the table?

ANSWER: Two racks of baby back pork ribs. And maybe some cole slaw.

QUESTION: Do you think you could set aside your personal beliefs to represent all of the people?

ANSWER: Absolutely. We are all Americans. We believe we all have a say in how our nation is run. Even the majority.

QUESTION: What are your thoughts on engaging our military in other people's wars?

ANSWER: We say everyone on *The View* should fight her own battles.

QUESTION: If you were a tree, what kind of a tree would you be?

ANSWER: That's the stupidest question we've ever heard. Next.

FRONT PORCH
POLITICS

One thing has always bugged us about the first family's lodgings: The White House has a beautiful porch, but other than a nice photo op setting, it never gets used.

Look through the history books, and we bet you won't find a single picture of a Commander-in-Chief sitting in a Cracker Barrel rocking chair fanning himself on the front porch of the White House. Why is that? Why isn't our president taking advantage of all that square footage that we, the taxpayers, are paying for?

Let's face it, we all need a little down time, even presidents. What better way to have that down time than sitting on a front porch swatting away flies? Or Senators. Maybe the office of the president wouldn't be so stressful if the porch was used for the purpose it was built. It's the perfect place for the residents of the White House to sit and reflect on the day's events. It's peaceful. There is no television, so the president wouldn't have to listen to the newscasters telling him what a terrible job he's doing. He could just sit there, drinking lemonade and waving to the tourists.

Bill and Hillary might have gotten along a little better while at the White House had there been a front porch swing for them to sit on in the evenings. Lincoln might have even passed on going to see a play that night if he and the Mrs. could have ordered up a mint julep and sat out front watching the sunset.

In our administration, that is how we plan to alleviate some of the stress that naturally goes with the job. We're going to have rocking chairs, a couple of fly swatters, and maybe even a floor fan with the cord stretching into the White House.

If the bugs (or Senators) get to be too much for us, we might even think about having the front porch screened in. It'll change the look of the place, but then what did all those concrete barriers do? We understand the need for added security, and keeping the mosquitoes away from our Commanders-in-Chief would be just as important.

The president and his family aren't the only ones who need to spend more time on the front porch. The whole nation does. As a modernized version of FDR's fireside chats, we might even broadcast our radio addresses from the front porch and encourage the country to listen from theirs. Who knows, families might start getting along better, neighbors might act more neighborly, and high blood pressure and stomach ulcers might become diseases of the past.

By the way, do you know there is even a Professional Porch Sitters Union? It was started by a guy named Claude Stephens, and it's made up of people who believe porch sitting is what is missing from society today. The union, headquartered in Lexington, Kentucky, has only one rule and it's also their slogan:

"Sit down a spell. That can wait."

The group doesn't have any future events planned, nor do they have mandatory meetings. The only thing they're about is relaxing on the front porch.

Can you imagine if the international community was to adopt an attitude like that? What would it do for world peace? Mahmoud Ahmadinejad might not be nearly so grumpy if he'd just spend a little more time on his front porch. Imagine Kim Jong Il out on his front porch, sipping a glass of sweet tea. It'd be a little hard to think about nuclear weapons then, wouldn't it?

We agree with Claude. People don't sit on their porches nearly enough these days just to shoot the breeze. We stay in our air-conditioned houses and sit comatose in front of our television sets or computer screens. Sometimes we don't even know when the sun goes down. Or rises.

Most of us hardly spend any time outside anymore. We come home from work and lock our doors behind us. We keep our kids in, our cars in our garages, and our lives safely secured away.

But don't you think when we all moved inside we lost a good portion of our sense of community?

A Rick and Bubba co-presidency will be dedicated to reversing this trend. Not only are we going to put rockers on the White House porch, we are going to place them in front of the Capitol Building, the Supreme Court, and all the other government buildings, too. When you think about it, the whole Lincoln Memorial is a front porch. Which president do you think looks the least stressed? Lincoln sitting down in his memorial, or Jefferson standing up in his? Lincoln, of course. All he needs is a good book to read.

Porch sitting is a good way to pass your life. Enjoying the moment. People who sit on their front porch are too relaxed to get fired up over anything. The stock market could be crashing, your enemies could be planning all sorts of evil against you, the housing bubble could be bursting, but if you're relaxing in your rocker on your front porch, all you'll say is "Well, well, well. . . ."

THE UNDERDOG WINS

We realize we are entering the race a little late, and we know that we are not Washington insiders. On the surface, both of those elements would appear to put us at a disadvantage.

But there is a theory that has existed in both politics and sports for years, and it is this: the underdog has the advantage. People naturally feel sorry for the guy at the bottom. That's why a sports team or a politician never wants to appear overly confident of a win, because that attitude will end up going against him or her. No one is really sure why or how this works, but time and again, Americans always root for the underdog.

We have both spent our lives perfecting the loser position. We are underdogs and proud of it. We know we could go to the gym every day and have six-pack abs, but we also know that being in shape could backfire on us in the long run. That's why we eat whatever we want and don't do a lot of exercise. We are exercise underdogs.

We also know that we could have the brains of Bill Gates, but we didn't want that to backfire on us either. That's why we chose not to graduate summa cum laude. It had nothing to do with our grade point average. It was our choice to hold ourselves back year after year after year. Do you think it was easy to maintain our underdog academic advantage throughout our entire collegiate life and beyond?

When people see the shape we're in, or they hear about one of the messes we've somehow gotten ourselves into, they feel sorry for us. We win the pity vote hands down.

If it takes the pity vote to get us to sweep the nation come Election Day and win the co-presidency, then so be it. We have no problem looking pitiful.

In fact, most people tell us it's our best side.

REALITY CHECK

Some programs and policies within our government haven't worked out as our leaders had hoped. Pretending not to see how badly a program has failed hasn't helped our country very much either. When we make a mistake by passing a certain bill, or changing a certain law, or interpreting the Constitution in a way it was never intended to be interpreted, then why can't we just say "Whoops" and start over? It's no big deal. Everyone makes mistakes. There is no shame in confessing we blew it.

But some people can't admit the obvious. It's like the story of a dog named Lucky. Lucky, a German Shepherd guide dog for the blind, lives somewhere in Germany. His work record is 0 for 4, meaning that apparently Lucky has had four different opportunities to prove he is capable of doing his job as a guide dog, and four times he has come up short.

In spite of his track record, however, Lucky's trainers have taken out yet another ad stating that the dog is available for placement. *Did you catch the fact that Lucky is 0 for 4 on his job resumé?* You would think that a guide dog's track record would mean something, wouldn't you? Sort of like personal references in the human world. But apparently those around Lucky couldn't admit the obvious.

Let's review Lucky's employment history in detail. According to reports, Lucky led his first owner in front of a bus. Now, even if we were to excuse this as Lucky simply having a bad fur day, his second owner might disagree . . . if he could. He can't, because Lucky led his second owner off the end of a pier. His third owner didn't fare much better. Lucky allegedly gave him a nudge, knocking him off a railway platform just in time to catch the Frankfurt Express the hard way. That owner died, too. Lucky walked his fourth owner into heavy traffic and left him there where the owner (not Lucky . . . he was too smart to remain in the middle of the street) was promptly hit by a vehicle and killed.

Once again, do the math, that's a zero percent success rate. If these reports are true, wouldn't you say it's time to retire ol' Lucky? We think so, but apparently Lucky's owners disagree. Lucky is in the employment line waiting for his next assignment. And get this—the prospective employers won't be told of Lucky's work history because Lucky's owners are afraid if the dog senses nervousness around him (and who wouldn't get nervous around Lucky), he might do something "silly."

You think?

And what does Lucky have to do with our government? Sometimes government can work the same way. We keep doing the same things over and over in spite of the fact that they failed miserably the last time, and the time before that, and the time before that. (Raising taxes to help the economy comes to mind.)

Some politicians keep refusing to accept the obvious, and then they want us to keep re-electing them so they can try their failed programs again. Amazingly, we vote them back in even though they've led us off the end of a pier, into traffic, in front of a bus, and in front of a speeding train, figuratively speaking. No matter what they do, we keep returning them to office.

Other than Lucky and politicians, where else would we ever put up with this kind of "overlooking the obvious"? If a pilot was 0 for 4 in his landings, would he keep his job? What about a surgeon? Or a New York City cab driver? Of course not. We're pretty sure a New York City cab driver has to have at least a 1 in 4 standing to stay employed.

Maybe Lucky should retire from his guide-dog job and be satisfied with being somebody's pet. If you've been responsible for the death of four blind people, maybe it's time to reevaluate your skills in the guide dog industry. Maybe being a guide dog just isn't your calling.

But then again, maybe the dog is smarter than us all. Maybe he's some kind of double agent. Maybe Lucky is just pretending to be a guide dog, but what he's really doing is trying to get back at all of us humans.

Or maybe it's something else. Maybe Lucky has some deep-seated issues. *"I vil take you into traffic and I vil abandon you. And you vil like it!"*

Maybe Lucky needs to see a dog psychiatrist. Or go on *Dr. Phil.*

As to whatever is going on in Lucky's head, we can only speculate. All we know is that under our administration, we're going to always try to see the obvious.

And reject any green card applications for Lucky.

RICK AND BUBBA
ARE IN THE HOUSE

We have to confess. One of the main reasons that we are seeking the co-presidency of the United States isn't really all that noble. If the truth be told, it's because we heard there are two kitchens in the White House. Frankly, we cannot think of a greater incentive to move our families all the way to Washington. We could each build our own house with two kitchens, but since we've already spent the advance money from our first, second, and third books, moving to 1600 Pennsylvania Avenue where double kitchens already exist seems like the best solution.

Before you can move to the White House, you have to run for office and the country has to elect you. You can't just show up one day with a U-Haul. First, there are all those concrete barriers in front of the place now. It's hard to get a moving van past those. There's also the Secret Service and a first lady who might not be too happy with someone just showing up unannounced and wanting to move in. First ladies can be possessive when it comes to the White House. Remember Hillary when Bill's term was up? She didn't want to leave. Most of our first ladies have probably wanted to stay. Downsizing can be a pain. I'm sure after we serve out our term, Betty and Sherri aren't going to be in any rush to leave the White House either.

So it's understandable why Hillary, Nancy, Barbara, Laura, and any other first lady wouldn't have wanted to see a U-Haul come barreling up the driveway before they had a chance to make a graceful exit.

That's why we're doing it the proper way: running for office and giving everyone fair warning.

Since there are two kitchens and two of us, we figure we'll each take one. It's simple math. The larger kitchen, we understand, is the one in the basement. We'll draw straws to see which one of us gets that one. The basement kitchen is used most often for the big White House dinner parties. We're not sure where the White House barbeque is located, but we could probably share that. The barbeque will be used for our more elite guests, like the Queen of England. The Queen looks like she could use a good barbeque. That could be why there's always so much turmoil in the royal family. No barbeques.

Aside from the two kitchens, there are a lot of other rooms in the White House. As we've already noted, some one hundred thirty-two rooms in all. (Apparently, staff members with way too much time on their hands counted them one day.) Under a dual presidency, we would each get sixty-six rooms. That's sixty-six rooms for the Bussey family and sixty-six rooms for the Burgess family. Finally, all the Burgess kids will get to have their own bedroom!

My (Rick) wife Sherri likes to host class parties, so we would probably do a lot of that sort of thing. We'd have plenty of sleepovers, too. (After the Clinton administration, can you still have sleepovers at the White House? We'll have to look into that one.)

If elected, I would also want to hold my class reunion at the White House. This would not be at the taxpayer's expense, of course. I just want to use the facility for the event, that's all. Maybe hang a disco ball from the ceiling of the Oval Office. (I believe Bill Clinton might have done this on occasion, too. And Lyndon Johnson's daughter had her prom at the White House, so it's not like I would be setting any precedents.)

Think about it—we all dream of going to our class reunions and being able to flaunt the fact that we've made it in life. We want to be able to say that we're a doctor, a successful businessperson, a professional actor, or something that would impress all those people who wouldn't give us the time of day back in high school. What better way to do that than to say you're co-president of the United States? No one else is going to have that written on a name tag. (Except for Bubba—but he didn't go to my high school anyway.)

I don't even care if our term doesn't fall on the regular fifteen- or twenty-year reunion times. I would still hold the reunion during our administration. It could be a sixteen-year reunion, an eighteen-and-a-half-year reunion, or perhaps even a twenty-one-year-and-four-months reunion. I don't care. All I know is if I'm co-president, I am going to hold my high school reunion on the grounds. Every girl who wouldn't go with me to the prom is getting a personal invitation . . . exactly one week after the event.

What I (Bubba) am going to enjoy most about living in the White House is that secret tunnel where they say you can walk out of the White House and end up across the street. This is one of the main incentives for me running for president. I want to be able to live in a place where I can sneak out and go get ice cream. I want to find a good Baskin Robbins within jogging distance of the White House (I only said jogging to see if you were paying attention) and visit it every night after dinner.

Have you ever noticed how ice cream puts everyone in a good mood? Ice cream is a natural anti-depressant. When's the last time you heard an ice cream truck playing with "Alone Again, Naturally"? Ice cream trucks play happy tunes. They want to cheer you up, not bring you down.

Portsmouth, Virginia, had an ordinance banning ice cream trucks from playing their tunes, but it was eventually overturned. City attorneys decided that the ice cream truck owners had a legal right to play their music. Good for them. We need more happy music in our lives. And we could all use more ice cream.

Once, at a loan closing that Betty and I were involved in, the parties had a slight disagreement, and eventually one side got up and walked out. I forget now what the matter was even about, but I decided to go out and buy everybody some ice cream. When I came back and started handing out ice creams, everyone lightened up and the closing went smoothly after that.

Ice cream has that kind of power.

Has anyone ever thought that when North Korea's Kim Jong Il throws his hand up in the air for a photo, maybe he's just trying to say, "Double scoop over here"?

THE NOT-SO-SECRET SERVICE

We understand the need to have a Secret Service that protects our president and his family. Our issue is only with the "secret" part of it. We wonder just how secret it can be when they're dressed in those Armani suits and sunglasses, with a wire hanging out of their ear.

When we take office, one of the first things we're going to do is change the uniform of the Secret Service. They're going to khakis and a tank top. If we're making a speech on August 12th anywhere in the South or the Northeast, we don't want our Secret Service passing out from the heat. As long as they are trained killers (and very good babysitters for our kids), we don't care how casually they dress.

Another thing we will do is put a lot of our relatives in this position. No one protects you like family. You think the Kennedys have nepotism? Nepotism will reach an all-time high under the Burgess/Bussey administration. The Washington A-list will never get out of the Bs.

We would like to address another point, too. We realize that the public under our Constitution has the right to protest. But as co-presidents, we would also like to exercise our right not to hear them. If anyone is protesting us, or spitting at us, or heckling us in any way, we will give our Secret Service the authority to tackle them down, hog-tie 'em, and then say, "Does anyone else have anything to say?" It might sound a little rough, but it works. I (Rick) saw that technique used at a football game once, and I've never forgotten it. The officials announced that no one was allowed to come down onto the field and rush the goal posts during the game, but some fans did it anyway. The security guards handled it beautifully, though. They just walked out onto the field and hog-tied one of the offenders and laid him on the twenty-yard line. Then, they looked up into the stands and said, "Anyone else want to try that?"

Strangely enough, no one did.

Again, sometimes being president is just a matter of looking at what works historically.

ROYAL PROTOCOL

We realize that any sitting president is going to have to entertain royalty on occasion. It just goes with the territory. Because of this, it is a good idea to be up on what the proper protocol is for greeting and dining with royalty.

We've done our homework. First, when you greet the Queen of England, you are to refer to her as Your Majesty, or Ma'am. You should never say, "Hey, girlfriend."

Likewise, when addressing Prince Charles, you are expected to say "Your Royal Highness." You would not, as we might do in the South, say "How's your momma?" The Queen Mother is not "Momma."

It is your own choice whether you bow, curtsy, or simply shake hands. For any of our relatives meeting the Queen at one of our White House dinners, we would recommend shaking hands. But royal protocol demands that you remove the black olives from each of your fingers first.

Also, never slap the Queen on the back as a greeting unless she happens to be choking. The Queen is not a "good ol' boy." If she does happen to be choking, you should bow or curtsy first and then apply the Heimlich maneuver.

According to protocol, a meal with the Queen should never last more than one hour and forty-five minutes, and it should contain a maximum of three courses. Now, right there is why it is better to be a president than royalty. Only three courses? Where is the honor in that?

It is our understanding that members of the royal family like to eat the typical food and drink of whatever region they happen to be in. If they visit the White House during our administration, it will be barbeque. There will be no special treatment for royalty at a White House barbeque, either. It'll be a "first grab, first served" affair. If the Queen desires to distinguish herself by wearing a pig hat, that's fine. But it's still every man (and woman) for himself.

THE SUPREMES . . .
COURT, THAT IS

Oyez! Oyez! Oyez! (That's French for "Hear ye! Hear ye! Hear ye!" or "More oysters at Table Six." We're not sure.)

It also happens to be the call to begin each session of the Supreme Court.

One question that is often asked of presidential candidates is who, if given the opportunity, they would nominate to the Supreme Court. The first person that comes to our minds is Judge Judy. We believe our nation would greatly benefit from Judge Judy's no-nonsense approach to the judicial system. Frankly, we'd love to see her climb right over the bench and slap someone, or hear her put some arrogant attorney in his place with, *"Hey, hey, HEY! I'm the judge and don't you be popping off to me!"*

That's the number-one thing that's wrong with our judicial system today—it's not entertaining enough. More and more courtroom cases are being televised, while fewer and fewer of them make for good television. Supreme Court cases can be the worst. The attorneys present their arguments, the justices deliver their opinions and ruling, and then they move on to their next case. Where's the excitement? Where's the *"Do you see 'Stupid' written on my forehead?"* or *"Don't look up at God, look at me!"* and other famous Judge Judy quotes? Think about it—can you remember a single Ruth Ginsberg quote? Or one of David Souter's? We didn't think so.

We're reasonably certain we'll need to come up with a few more nominees besides Judge Judy. We've seen the pictures of the Supreme Court, and from what we can tell it's likely there will be a few more vacancies coming up soon. What is the average age of a Supreme Court justice anyway? 106? And that's the average of the junior members. Not that we're against men and women working well into their golden years. We think that's great. We plan to work long after our demise, too. (. . . wonder if we'll still be doing our radio show when we're in our nineties and beyond. We doubt it. Not that we wouldn't want to do one. It's just that by then the powers that be will probably say we're irrelevant to the younger generation. Irrelevant? We'll be wearing baggy pants, the biggest activity of our day will be falling asleep in front of the television set, and our hair will probably be some funny shade of orange or blue. And they'll say we're irrelevant to the younger generation? That's impossible. We'll look just like them!)

I (Rick) believe my mother would be another good choice to serve on the Supreme Court. When I was growing up, she was always pretty good at handing out the justice at our house. The only problem was it wasn't blind justice. She had twenty-twenty vision in front, in the back of her head, and a pair of eyes on each side, too.

My mother would love serving on the Supreme Court. What mother wouldn't? To have the absolute, undisputed, final say in every situation, with no possible chance of appeal? Isn't that a mother's dream?

Other than Judge Judy and my mother, we'll still need to have a few more names. But it's not easy. We can see why the process is so difficult for sitting presidents. Other government positions can be given to your old college buddies, relatives, or your most enthusiastic supporters. But when it comes to the Supreme Court, you have to really think about it. You can't just say "I nominate, Greg 'The Bull' Olson . . . he'll be great for some laughs!" Nor can you make Bruce Springsteen a Supreme Court justice just because you like his music.

A Supreme Court nominee has to have the wisdom of Solomon. He or she needs to know the law (preferably more than the phone number of a local bail bondsman), and most of all, be a scholar of Constitutional law. Despite what a few of the judges have thought over the years, their job isn't to legislate. Their job is to interpret the Constitution, so they need to know it inside and out.

But Supreme Court justices can't be all brains. They need to understand the common person, too. We should have a few people on the High Court who have actually been to a Wal-Mart lately. How can we expect the Supreme Court to hand down fair rulings that are going to affect the whole nation if they've never eaten at McDonald's? They need to eat at the places we eat, shop at the places we shop, and vacation at Disney World. If some of them don't lead the lives of ordinary men and women, how are they going to know what we're thinking? Not that public opinion should sway their judgments in any way. That's not what we're saying. As we said, the Supreme Court answers to the Constitution. But it still wouldn't hurt to catch a glimpse of a judicial robe every now and then as it turns down the canned food aisle, would it?

That is why if we're elected, we intend to help the Supreme Court improve its public image. They look a little stuffy to us. And their photographs always look the same. Don't get us wrong, we have nothing against the robes. We've both been in church choirs ourselves. But you don't see us wearing our robes at our local supermarket.

Have you noticed they never seem to smile either? Why is that? You hardly ever see a picture of a Supreme Court justice smiling or laughing. A few of them don't seem to have a sense of humor at all (a certain Ms. Ginsberg comes to mind). But how can they rule the way they've ruled on some cases and not laugh?

MERRY CHRISTMAS
FROM DC!

Traditionally, the president and his wife hold an annual Christmas tree lighting ceremony. It is a festive and much anticipated occasion for the Washington community, as well as for the entire nation. No matter what else is happening around the world, our nation takes this moment to stop and reflect on the spirit and beauty of the holiday celebration and what it means to each one of us.

This is just one more reason to elect us. If you look at the other candidates (those who've dropped out and those still in the race), what kind of a Christmas tree are you likely to have? John Edwards's tree will lean a little too far to the left. Hillary Clinton's tree will lean whichever way the wind is blowing.

But we know how to pick a Christmas tree. Our Christmas tree lighting ceremony will be the best this nation has ever witnessed. If my (Bubba) wife Betty Bussey has anything to say about it, we won't have just one Christmas tree at the White House. We'll have dozens! Once again, in the interest of full disclosure, I have to confess that Betty is a Christmas tree addict. She has been battling this addiction for years, but so far she has been helpless against it. We tried an intervention once and managed to get her to cut back to just one tree and a couple of wreaths. But the following year, she was back to her old ways.

When it comes to decorating pines, Douglas firs, and anyone who happens to be standing too close and too still, Betty Bussey has no willpower.

She's quick, too. She can have a Christmas tree up and fully decorated in minutes. In fact, we've often wondered if Betty isn't part elf. To Betty it's not Christmas until she has created a virtual winter wonderland throughout our entire home. It's amazing. I'm not talking those short two- or three-foot tree tops that pass themselves off as a real tree either. These trees are eight and nine feet tall. She'll even decorate a smaller tree for each of our kids' bedrooms.

Now when I say Betty fully decorates a tree, I mean she *fully decorates a tree*. You have to get this image. Every branch will have lights on it, along with an ornament hanging from the end of it. *Every* single branch. The lights aren't just haphazardly strewn on the branches either. They're intricately woven around them. Up until now, presidents and first ladies have only played at Christmas decorating. Betty will leave them all behind in elf dust.

The speed with which Betty goes through the house decorating isn't human.

I've never seen anyone move that fast. I'm sure Washington hasn't either. Not a lot moves fast there.

But don't think Rick and I won't be helping Betty out with the decorating. When it's time to turn on the lights, we'll be more than happy to flip the timer.

The Rick and Bubba White House Christmas Letter

So confident are we that we are going to be elected co-presidents, we have gone ahead and written our very first White House Christmas Letter. We wanted to give you, our faithful supporters, the first look at it here.

As you read through the following, please catch any typos that you see. (We're not in the Oval Office yet and can't afford the luxury of a proof-reader.) You may notify us of any corrections at:

Rick and Bubba
1600 Pennsylvania Avenue
Washington DC 20500

(The White House staff should be more than happy to hold our mail until we officially arrive.)

MERRY CHRISTMAS FROM DC!

Here is our first presidential Christmas letter . . .

Dear Fellow Americans:

It is hard to believe that our first year in office is already nearing its end. It has been a good year, and by all accounts a successful one. We didn't promise to do a single thing in office, and so far, we can proudly say that we have lived up to that promise.

It isn't easy to sit in the Oval Office day after day without anything on our To-Do list. But we have proven it can be done. We flew by the seat of our ample pants and took things as they came up, one issue at a time.

We have brought the Democrats and the Republicans in Congress together like no previous administration has been able to do. Both sides of the aisle equally regret the day that we took office. If that isn't unity, we don't know what is.

Rogue nations are once again treating America with respect. Our plan to prove how serious and well equipped we are by taking over a small country, one that wouldn't put up much of a fight, say like France, has worked out great. It has kept the world on its toes and given us an endless supply of croissants.

In the past, other countries have been able to count on a certain amount of restraint, predictability, and levelheadedness from America's leaders. But ever since we came into office, that predictability is gone because we refuse to be put into a box. We don't want the world knowing what we're going to do from one moment to the next. We prefer to keep everyone guessing. Why should Kim Jong Il get to throw all the tantrums? Let the world wonder what America is up to for a change.

So, this Christmas as you hang your stocking over your fireplace or wherever you happen to hang it, remember that you have a lot to be thankful for and virtually nothing to worry about now that we're in office. Unless, of course, you're French. In which case, hey, it was all just a joke. As soon as we get out of office, we plan on giving France back. But not the croissants.

Merry Christmas from the White House,
Your co-presidents, Rick and Bubba,
and our lovely first ladies

SKELETONS IN
OUR CLOSETS

Remember Gary Hart and his boat trip with Donna Rice? Or President George W. Bush and his decades-old DUI arrest? Or how about President Clinton and his "I didn't inhale" confession?

Presidential candidates can have their past, present, and sometimes even their trash gone through with a fine-toothed comb. Kindergarten time-outs can even come up in a debate. So those who run for office have to think of everything they'll need to disclose because there is no telling what lengths an opponent or enemy will go to in an attempt to discredit them. Some politicians have had more skeletons popping up during their campaign than in *Halloween III*.

For me (Rick), Panama City in the 1980s alone should be enough to keep me from the White House. But that was a long time ago. I am a different person today, and most Americans are good forgivers. (The honest ones know they have their own baggage to be forgiven of, too.)

In the interest of full disclosure, however, we feel we should go ahead and confess a few of our other skeletons . . .

I (Rick) once almost got into a fight with the music group Air Supply. It was backstage at one of their concerts. I don't know if I'm more embarrassed about almost getting into the fight, or about saying I was at an Air

Supply concert. But back then I was a fan of the group. "I'm All Out of Love" still rings in my head to this day. Not by choice. It just does.

But back to my confession: My connection with Air Supply came when I was in college and was asked to work security for one of their concerts. It sounded like a cool job, so I took it. But then, backstage when the drummer started complaining about a hurt toe, I couldn't help but offer what little medical advice I knew. "Hey, man, why don't you just suck it up?" I said. I might have said it in Latin, you know, to sound more like a real doctor. I'm not sure. Either way, I think he wasn't very happy. The next thing I knew the entire group had surrounded me. (Just so you know, Air Supply is a lot tougher than one might think.)

Obviously, I did manage to escape, but from then on, I've tried to keep my medical advice to myself.

Another thing I should probably confess is that I (please don't think I'm letting you down, guys. I'm just trying to be honest here) actually enjoy Broadway musicals. Whenever Sherri and I go to one, I pretend I don't want to be there, that I'm only going for her and our daughter. But the truth is I really do enjoy them. Tucked away somewhere in the dark crevices of our home, if anyone wanted to do the searching, they would find actual Broadway playbills. Several of them. My favorite playbill is for the Broadway musical *Cats*.

Okay, there, I've said it. Hold that against me if you want, but it's the truth. I'll even go further. I'm not ashamed to admit that I cry every time the old cat sings "Memories."

But should that keep me out of the White House? Should I be discriminated against just because I shed a few tears over a cat and his song of lament? Don't we want a president who's in touch with his inner musical?

Another confession I have to make is that at one time I actually coached Little League soccer. I know I might have alluded to soccer being a Communist plot, but let me explain. For the record, I had full intentions of only using my football-loving presence, as well as a few football terms, in an attempt to turn the game around and make it a sport we could all be proud of. But I got sucked in and became a lot more involved in the game than I should have. I'm sure that today pictures still exist of me on the field coaching the kids and perhaps even playing an actual game of soccer. I realize this fact is letting a lot of you down, but I hope you'll find it in your heart to overlook this little indiscretion when you enter the voting booth this November.

I (Bubba) have something that I need to come clean on, too. It goes back a few years, but I might as well get it off my chest and beat our opponents to the punch: I don't eat white food. I don't mean food made by Caucasian cooks; I'm talking about the actual color of the food. Especially cole slaw.

You see, when I was in the first grade, I accidentally dropped a lunch tray on the cafeteria floor one day. The rather large lunch lady yelled at me in front of everyone and handed me a mop to clean it up. I was embarrassed, but when I looked down at my shoe and saw a glob of cole slaw was now stuck to it, I was mortified. There is no way to look cool with cole slaw on your sneakers. To this day, I have a fear of cole slaw. And large lunch ladies. And, of course, white food.

Skeletons or not, we hope you'll give us a chance to prove that we can rise above the skeletons of the past, live today to its fullest, build toward the future . . . and keep the cole slaw off our shoes.

PRESIDENTIAL DENIALS

A politician's life can be, well, unpredictable. Because of this, we figured it might be a good idea for us to go ahead and make all of our denials ahead of time. Here are just a few that we're working on:

"We did not trade guns for hostages. We traded guns for sausages."

"We know nothing about Watergate. We know about watermelon. But it doesn't have a gate."

"We have never been on a yacht named Monkey Business with anyone named Donna Rice. We don't like monkeys and we didn't even know Condoleezza had a sister."

"We would never expose undercover CIA agents for political reasons. For dinner, yes, but for political reasons, never!"

"We know nothing about Haliburton. We have, however, been treated for halitosis on occasions."

"Whitewater? We did go rafting once."

"Plagiarism? We're quoting plagiarists. That's not plagiarism."

"We did not inhale. If we had, the pants would have fit."

"We don't know what we knew when we didn't know that we knew it or how we knew it or whether we really even knew it at all, know what we mean?"

"We did not have a plate of pork ribs with that woman."

GOVERNMENT WASTE

Start trimming the fat, America!

Really, we mean it. Of course, you need to read on to find out which type of fat we're calling you to trim. Not the cellulite kind.

We're speaking, of course, of government fat. Do you realize there is a government program that pays American farmers some $2 billion every year NOT to farm their land? That's like paying the two of us not to eat. Farmers should do what they do—farm. We should do what we do—eat what they farm.

The government's position on this doesn't make much sense to us. Why are we paying someone not to do their job? Talk about a government program gone amuck! Doesn't that sound like a big waste of taxpayer money? Sure, we pay some members of Congress to go to Washington and not work, but that's different.

You won't believe it, but there are other examples of government waste. According to one report, congressional investigators received $55,000 in federal student loan funding for a fictional college that they created to test the Department of Education. Now, many of us have known people who received a diploma from a fictional college, but taxpayers aren't footing the bill for them. We both go to a fictional gym, but we don't expect the government to pay for that either.

When it comes to how taxpayer money is being spent, we the people have got to start speaking up. For starters, why don't we come up with an alternative fuel source that can be made from farm produce and then pay farmers to grow that? If farmers were growing soybeans and those soybeans were being turned into alternative fuel, we wouldn't be in such a vulnerable position when dealing with oil-rich countries. This seems like a good idea to us, and it's certainly making much better use of the soybean than turning it into tofu burgers. At least this way, the soybean would get to keep its dignity.

Another study revealed that some federal employees were abusing their government-issued credit cards and charging personal items on them, such as cruises, Ozzie Osborne tickets, tattoos, and more. We don't know about you, but we don't want our taxpayer dollars paying for some government employee's tattoo. How can you ever repossess a tattoo?

It was also discovered that between the years of 1997 and 2003, the Department of Defense had apparently failed to get their (rather, *our*) money back on a hundred million dollars of fully refundable, unused airline tickets. The government also double paid for some twenty-seven thousand airline tickets, meaning that they paid for the original ticket, but then also reimbursed the passenger for the cost of the ticket. We realize paperwork is a pain, but even more we realize that we as taxpayers need to be more vigilant regarding what's happening to the money we send to Washington.

Our administration will do its best to rid our government of this kind of blatant waste. We will stand up against pork barrel spending. Pork rinds are fine, as is ham and, of course, SPAM. But we draw a line in the sand at all this pork barrel stuff.

Another area where we find government waste is in staffing. How much staff does one politician need anyway? We do a nationally syndicated show that is heard in about fifty markets, we sell our own merchandise, run our own Web site that offers many services, and we deal with fifty different sales teams, fifty different promotional teams, several advertising clients, as well as do speaking engagements and write books, all with a regular staff of five. Come on, a politician doesn't need to employ a small town to keep track of all the congressional votes he misses. To those of us on the outside looking in, it appears that a portion of these staffers are simply being paid to stand around and look good.

Some politicians have too many cars, too. When I (Rick) see a politician pulling up to an event leading a caravan of ten or so vehicles, I think, what's that all about? Security? That's not security. If it was for security, they'd be forming a circle around the politician's car, like they did in the Old West days. A line of cars doesn't offer security. A line is a parade—at the taxpayer's expense. We don't need ten cars following John Kerry. John might need a few extra cars to carry his money, but he doesn't need ten. He could leave the rest of it at home.

We've got to get the federal budget under control again. Someone needs to be watching the cookie jar. That's another reason why we're running for the co-presidency.

We don't mean to brag, but cookie jars are our specialty.

PRESIDENTIAL SOUND BITES

Throughout history, our leaders have provided us with some memorable sound bites. Here are just a few of them:

"I am a Ford. Not a Lincoln."

—Gerald Ford

"Being president is like running a cemetery: you've got a lot of people under you and nobody's listening."

—Bill Clinton

"I did think it was effective when I weaved in stories of real people in the audience and their everyday challenges. Like the woman here tonight whose husband is about to lose his job. She's struggling to get out of public housing and get a job of her own. Hillary Clinton, I want to fight for you."

—Al Gore

"But there are advantages to being elected President. The day after I was elected, I had my high school grades classified Top Secret."

—Ronald Reagan

"If you could kick the person in the pants responsible for most of your trouble, you wouldn't sit for a month."

—Theodore Roosevelt

"I have had a lot of adversaries in my political life, but no enemies that I can remember."

—Gerald Ford

"An enemy generally says and believes what he wishes."

—Thomas Jefferson

"Governments tend not to solve problems, only to rearrange them."

—Ronald Reagan

"It's a very good question, very direct, and I'm not going to answer it."

—George H. W. Bush

If we are going to sit in the Oval Office, we will be expected to come up with our own words of wisdom. We have given this a lot of thought, and here is a small sampling of some of the sound bites that you can expect from us:

"We have seven children between us. We can deal with Congress."

"Yes, our wives are really running this country. And we're man enough to admit it."

"America is the land of opportunity, not guarantees."

"Rogue nations beware—we have so many nukes we can't count them all, and we're not afraid to use them. Have a nice day."

"It's okay to remember your past, but don't let it hinder your future."

"Never in the history of time has a country taxed itself into prosperity."

"You can read our lips. But don't get in the way of our eating."

THE PRESIDENTIAL LIMOUSINE

We've never been in the presidential limousine, but we assume it must have a good snack bar. If it doesn't, once elected we're going to have one installed, along with high definition television. We'd also like to operate a ham radio station from the presidential limo. This is a longtime hobby of ours, and we think it would be a hoot to do it from the presidential limo. Has any other president ever done this? We don't think so. We might even get the Queen of England to call in on it every once in a while. She may secretly even have her own handle already. Who knows?

We also plan to paint the presidential limo a nice camouflage. That way, you'd never know when the president was visiting Wisconsin during hunting season, and for two dedicated hunters like us, that would be a good thing. We don't need the press scaring away the game.

As presidents, we're going to need our getaway times, where no one but our wives know where we are. The camouflage limo, as well as the underground tunnel out of the White House, will help that. We can sneak off whenever we want and go on a hunting trip.

We're not sure how the limo would look with a pair of buck antlers fastened across the front grill, but in honor of hunters everywhere, we would be willing to give it a try. Actually, the look might go nicely with the camouflage paint job.

We also think that a couple of crimson tide 'Bama banners would look pretty good waving in the wind from the antenna. Being president shouldn't mean you have to give up your team loyalty, should it? We realize we're supposed to represent all of the people, but during football season, too?

In addition to the Alabama banners, we thought we'd slap a few Rick and Bubba radio show bumper stickers to the front and rear fenders. We're only going to be in office a maximum of eight years, and we've got to make that time work for us.

Other than the above, we think we'll be happy with the presidential limousine. We know our kids will be. Can you imagine the look on their friends' faces when we start driving the neighborhood carpool in that!

TERM LIMITS

Should the nation actually elect us its first co-presidents, there is a matter that will need to be discussed on a national level. Over lunch, preferably.

The question is this: With two presidents, would the limit of two terms apply, or would a dual presidency qualify us for four terms (two apiece) for a total of sixteen years? It is uncharted waters, and there is no right or wrong answer yet. We just wanted to open it up for debate, so we can make our plans accordingly. If we're going to be gone from Birmingham sixteen years, we're going to need to get someone to pick up our mail.

We have already stated that people in Washington tend to remain there far too long, and we still hold to that opinion. Because of this, we assure you now that if we haven't done the "nothing" that we promised in our campaign in the four or eight years that we're in office, we will not stay on another two terms and waste even more taxpayer money.

But let's talk a little more about term limits. First of all, the concept of term limits is not about age. A lot of seventy- and eighty-year-olds have more wisdom in their little fingers than most of us have in our entire body. (We know you can't really have wisdom in a little finger, but go with us on this.) Our problem isn't how old a politician is. If a person runs for office at seventy, more power to him or her. It's not the age; it's the length of stay. It's basically about how many years we have to look at him or her on the evening news.

Term limits are good things. It might be nice to impose a few limits in other areas of life, too. What if we had them on celebrities? What if there was a limit on how many political comments one celebrity could make at awards ceremonies, and once he or she hit that number, he or she could only say "Thank you very much" and step down (and no ribbons allowed!). Or what about limits to scandals? Once an athlete, musician, or movie star is featured on the cover of one of those magazines at the grocery store checkout line more than five times in five months for anything involving drugs or alcohol abuse, out-of-wedlock pregnancies, co-habitating with his or her new boyfriend or girlfriend, family feuds, or shaving his or her head, he or she is banned from media attention for a minimum of three years. Let some others have some fun. Surely there are more troubled celebrities out there to choose from. With this rule, names like Paris Hilton, Britney Spears, and Lindsay Lohan would be bittersweet memories by now. And limits could apply to regular folks, too. Consider DMV workers. What if they were only allowed a limit of ten instances of filing their nails instead of opening their window? We could go on and on. The bottom line is that limits can dramatically improve job and life performance.

But don't worry. We don't want to be in Washington sixteen years. Like we've already said, when our four- or eight-year term is up we're going home. And on our drive back to Alabama, we might even drop off a few other politicians in their home states, too.

SUNRISE, SUNSET

If elected, we will put an end to Daylight Savings Time. No more of this "springing forward" or "falling back" craziness. Hawaii, Arizona, and parts of Indiana don't do it, so why are the rest of us continuing to put up with this insanity?

We feel it's high time for a change. If, after all this time, we still have to wait for a news reporter to tell us whether we're supposed to move our clocks ahead one hour or back one hour, the idea isn't working. Why don't we all just admit it and stop it?

The reason we can't seem to grasp the concept of Daylight Savings Time is simple: it doesn't make sense. We don't like doing things that don't make sense. We don't buy the fact that daylight savings gives us more daylight. It doesn't. We'd have more daylight even if we left our clocks alone. We would just have to get up earlier or stay up later to see it, but it would be there. The simple fact is, in the spring and summer months, we get more daylight. It has nothing to do with our clocks. It has to do with the rotation of the earth. Some months we're a little closer to the sun, other months we're a little farther away.

They say the original reason behind daylight savings time was to give children time to do their chores, like slopping the hogs or gathering the crops before they walked the two miles to school. How many kids in your neighborhood are slopping hogs and picking corn today? In fact, how many kids do you know who actually have chores? That's why it doesn't make sense. Who is Daylight Savings Time helping? We have to get up before dawn to get ready to do our morning radio talk show, but moving the clocks ahead an hour every spring doesn't make us feel any more like getting up.

Hate Daylight Savings Time? Elect us and you'll never have to reset your clocks again.

Unless the batteries die, of course, in which case, take it up with the bunny.

ONLY IN AMERICA

One part of a presidential candidate's bio is a listing of any awards that they've been given. Bubba and I have received a few throughout our careers, but the one that means the most to me is one that I received from an organization known as The Foundary. I guess you could say the honor has been burned into my memory. . . .

As I've already stated, I have made my share of poor choices in my life. But thanks to caring people, God's amazing grace, and a wife who believed in my future, I was able to get my life back on track. So much so that not long ago I was chosen by The Foundary to be the recipient of their annual Hope Award. Their rehabilitation program for people with drug or alcohol problems is based on what I believe is the most effective path to personal change and healing—a relationship with Jesus Christ. Since I had chosen this healing path, they wanted to acknowledge that and use me to help bring awareness that God can indeed change lives.

If you're familiar with the Bible at all, then you know that it is full of accounts of God using some broken and messed up people in amazing ways. God used broken people because that's all He had to choose from. We're all messed up in one way or another. Maybe it's an obvious addiction like alcohol, or maybe it's not so obvious like pride, greed, self-righteousness, or an unforgiving heart. Whatever our flaws, we all have them. (If you don't think you do, then that's your biggest flaw.)

I was both honored and humbled to be chosen for the Hope Award. I went through some difficult times a few decades ago when I temporarily lost my footing. I had some major disappointments in my life, and instead of picking myself up, moving on, and pouring all my energy into my future, I took the escape route of easing the pain the only way I knew how—alcohol. I discovered very quickly how destructive alcohol can be in someone's life. Did you know that some 82 percent of the people who get arrested are arrested for problems related to drugs and alcohol? Whenever we do a news story on the show where someone has done something stupid, we always look for the line in the report that says alcohol was involved.

But now, here I was, about to receive an award recognizing our radio show, our *New York Times* best-selling book, and most importantly, how my life has been changed through the love and grace of our Lord.

It was a special night. My wife, Sherri, was with me, as well as my mother. We had just finished the meal, and the program was in full swing. The speaker was giving a heart-wrenching talk about how God can and does change lives, including his own. People were crying, sniffling, wiping their noses; it was that kind of speech. Everyone in the room was hanging on his every word.

About that point is when things started to get interesting. (I realize that if we are elected to lead this country, we're going to have to learn how to act in situations like this. But at the time, we did the best we could under the circumstances.)

Sherri, wanting to see at what point the award would be handed out, picked up the printed itinerary and moved it closer to the lit candle on the table so she could read it. (Sherri should have followed William McKinley's campaign slogan of leaving well enough alone.)

As the speaker moved into one of the most painful stories of the night, and as I was trying to keep the lump in my throat under control, I turned ever so slightly and out of the corner of my eye I could see a flaming piece of paper now being waved wildly in the air. *Sherri had set the itinerary on fire!*

My mom and Sherri were now frantically trying to put out the flame. At the time, I didn't even know how the fire had started. I'm glad I didn't, because in most social circles, it's considered rude to be given an award and then set the table on fire. My hand couldn't reach that far across the table to be of any help, and I didn't want to disrupt the speech by yelling "Fire!" (That tends to draw the focus away from a speaker rather quickly.)

Finally, Sherri noticed a full glass of water next to her, so thinking quickly (a good trait for a first lady), she dumped the flaming paper into the water and extinguished the flame. There was just one problem. The speaker was in the middle of talking about drug abuse, and we were over at the table in a cloud of smoke, looking like we'd all just lit up.

With no itinerary now, I had no idea when I was supposed to go up on stage and receive my award. Sherri, bless her heart, got tickled over the incident (another good quality of a first lady) and couldn't stop laughing. My mother joined in, and now both women were giggling uncontrollably. I whispered to them that the story the speaker was sharing right then was very serious. I told them to regain their composure, but it was no use.

Finally, the speaker introduced me and I rose from out of the billow of smoke and walked up to the stage to receive my award. It was a beautiful award and one that I still cherish to this day. But rest assured, if I'm elected president and someday have the honor of receiving any other awards, candles will be strictly prohibited.

AIR FORCE ONE

One of the best things about being president will be getting to fly in Air Force One. Not because of the status of that great airplane, although we're sure it's impressive. It's because we're tired of the common man's air travel experience. It will be nice not to have to wait for landing clearance. You never hear of an air traffic controller saying, "Air Force One, you're number twenty-three in the line up. Kindly circle around the airport for another hour and a half."

Of course, once we're in office, we'll need to customize the aircraft to our liking. If it doesn't already have one, we are going to install an entire home theater system. We think it would be cool to watch the movie *Air Force One* while we're actually flying in Air Force One. It might be a little disappointing to realize that the escape hatch probably doesn't really exist, but it would still be cool.

I (Rick) would also need my *NCAA Football* video game on board, so I can play it in high definition. I think it would be fun to be the leader of the free world flying on Air Force One, and at the same time be quarterback of my favorite college team. Does life get any better than that?

Oh yeah—we also plan to install a giant pizza oven on the aircraft. We're sure they already have a fully equipped kitchen, but there probably isn't a giant pizza oven.

In addition to prohibiting individual bags of peanuts and four-count pretzels, we won't be stocking jelly beans on board. We love Ronald Reagan and believe he was one of the finest presidents our country has ever seen; but come on, Mr. President, *jelly beans?* Jelly beans are what you eat when you don't have any other choices. A lot of stores don't even carry them anymore. You have to buy them at special jelly bean stores. Do jelly beans really need their own store? Whose idea was this?

We will have ginger ale, though. Every airplane has to serve ginger ale, even Air Force One. It's a rule.

Another thing that would be cool about flying on Air Force One is that you get to bypass all the airport crowds. You never see the president of the United States running down those moving sidewalks, trying to catch his plane. The president gets a special landing strip where his motorcade pulls right up to the aircraft. That alone is worth running for office.

While we're on the subject of Air Force One, this might be a good time to bring up another matter. We would like to state for the record that we will not be flying to any far-off countries just to get a photo of us stepping off Air Force One in the blizzard of the century to greet some foreign dignitary. We don't mind meeting with the leaders of other countries, but it has to be in some place warm . . . like America. America has the best weather and more things to do and see than almost any other country. And we have Disney World. We can meet at the White House first, and then hop on Air Force One and continue the discussions in the land of Mickey Mouse. We're fairly certain that the president of the United States and his guests get an automatic line pass for all the rides.

After a full day of fun and nuclear proliferation talks, and dinner from our Air Force One pizza oven on the way home, can world peace be far behind?

CRIME
AND PUNISHMENT

If we are elected co-presidents, we will do our part to reduce crime in America . . . beginning with mailbox vandalism. Mailbox vandalism is an offense that has been growing across America and we intend to put a stop to this crime once and for all.

How many hard-working, unsuspecting Americans have driven home from their forty-eight-hour per week job only to discover that their mailbox has been blown to smithereens by some hooligan? Take a drive down any residential street in America, and chances are you will eventually come upon a mailbox that has been violated in this manner.

I have personally been a victim of mailbox assault too many times to count. I've had to undergo extensive therapy to even talk about it today. Aside from the counseling, what has helped me most is that I bought myself one of those indestructible mailboxes. This mailbox has gone through everything—vandals, birds making a pit stop on their flight south for the winter, the weight of first-of-the-month payment notices, you name it. The mailbox has handled it all without a single dent or the slightest sag. But with all my efforts, I hadn't factored in the possibility that my mail bunker could still get knocked off its pole. That was its weak point, and one night a ne'er do well discovered my new mailbox's Achilles' heel.

I was at baseball practice and was gone maybe a couple of hours at the most. When I returned, I couldn't help but notice that my mailbox, which had been upright when I left, was now on the ground, leaning up against its pole. In my fury I asked myself what kind of an animal could have done this. It was a blatant "in your face, what are you going to do about it?" bullying tactic. I had to respond or risk continued harassment.

Most normal mailbox crushers are middle-of-the-night thugs, sipping on gin and juice and doing their dastardly deeds in the cover of darkness. This guy had to have hit around seven o'clock in the evening. It was still light outside. What kind of a freak did I have on my hands? What kind of serial mailbox lunatic was going around disturbing our otherwise peaceful streets?

About that moment, I looked up and saw that a policeman had someone pulled over a few doors down. I thought, as any victim of this sort of crime would think, *Praise God, it's over*. I had been praying that this mailbox gang, this posse of postal pests, would be brought down and promptly arrested. Now, my prayers were being answered right before my eyes. Finally, one of the gang members had gotten a little too bold, too sloppy with his M.O. He had ventured out too early in the evening, and the law had nabbed him. I had a front-row seat to the whole good-versus-evil showdown.

Since the scene was taking place about two houses down from me, I drove down there. (Why waste steps?) I pulled up behind the police car. The policeman looked a little surprised when I rolled down my window and asked about the person he had pulled over and what they had done. (Note to self: policemen don't like you pulling up behind them and asking them what's going on.)

"I can't tell you that," he said.

I certainly understood his legal reasons for nondisclosure, but I had to know.

"Well," I said, "then let me ask you this: is it for knocking mailboxes down?"

He said, "No."

I figured whatever the guy did couldn't possibly have been as bad as the crime I was about to report to the officer. So I pressed on.

"Well, my mailbox a couple of houses down got knocked over. It had to have happened in the last two hours because I was here two hours ago. If we hurry, we can. . . ."

"You want me to come down there and check it out?" he said, matter-of-factly.

"Well, if you wouldn't mind."

He didn't budge. Obviously, he didn't share my urgency. But he did say, "Hey, you know what? We did just arrest a drunk on a ten-speed."

"A drunk on a ten-speed?"

"Yeah, maybe he's the perp." ("Perp," for those of you who don't watch *CSI*, is police talk for "bad guy.") "I'll come down and talk to you after we're done here."

Our perp was a drunk on a ten-speed? It wasn't exactly *Gangs of New York*, or even *West Side Story* without the dance numbers. But when the policeman finished up with what he was doing, he did indeed drive over to my house. I showed him the evidence—my mailbox that was now leaning up against the post. He didn't flinch. Obviously, he had been trained to show no fear. He just elaborated about the arrest.

"Awhile ago, we got a call that a person on a ten-speed was driving errat-ically down your street. When we got here, he was sitting on the side of the road holding his face. His cheeks were all puffed up, he was bleeding all over, but he was too dazed to tell us what happened. I bet he hit your mailbox. You, sir, probably saved his life."

"How's that?" I asked, not sure if he was being sincere or sarcastic.

"He was about to roll out there onto the main part of the road from your neighborhood, right into traffic. Your mailbox probably stopped him. He could've gotten himself killed."

"He had been drinking and driving a ten-speed?"

He nodded. "He's a repeat offender. Apparently, he's been in trouble for this sort of thing before. We got him on public intoxication."

Convinced that they had the guy in custody, I walked back into my house feeling vindicated. The mystery had been solved. Now all I had left to do was wonder if the perp would be sending me his medical bills for having my mailbox in his way. But that is a worry for another day. I had enough to concern me today.

Without a mailbox, I wasn't sure how I would get my fan mail now. "The same way you always do," Bubba said when I told him about the inci-dent. "Beg."

FIRST PITCH

One of the great traditions of our country, and one of the perks of the office of president, is that the president gets to throw out the ceremonial first pitch of the baseball season. President Taft started this custom back in 1910. We will, of course, be continuing it, except our pitches won't be those wimpy, try-not-to-hit-any-of-the-players kinds of pitches. Pitching the first ball of the season is the perfect time for a president to show his strength. You can't just let the baseball float over home plate like a Wiffle Ball. You have to throw it with everything you've got, and let the victims fall where they may. Gerald Ford understood this concept perfectly.

How sad has it been to watch some of our presidents, dressed in a suit, step onto the pitcher's mound and throw the baseball like an accountant? (If you're an accountant who is also a good baseball player, please overlook that last sentence.)

America wants a president who is strong, who knows how to pitch a baseball, and who knows the dress code of the ballpark. It's time to get a couple of world-class athletes in the Oval Office who, when called upon, can throw the ball like a man. This is just one more reason why we are answering the call to run for co-presidents of the United States.

For those of you who don't know, Bubba is an excellent baseball player. In fact, there was a time in his life when he considered going pro. Imagine the leader of the free world standing on the pitcher's mound and throwing a curve that could drop off the table? Bubba could do this.

Co-president Bubba Bussey would be the kind of ballplayer who would make the whole country proud on opening day of baseball season. He might even stay out there and play the rest of the game with the team.

Now we realize that some of you might be thinking to yourself that at our age, we are both better suited to walk out onto the mound and eat the first hot dog of the season. And you may be right. But perhaps we could do both.

I show my greatest strengths at bat. As your co-president, it will be an honor to hit Bubba's ceremonial pitch out of the ballpark.

If things go as we suspect they'll go, we might even start showing up at other sporting events. We could make the ceremonial first touchdown in the Super Bowl. We could hit the ceremonial first tennis ball in the US Open. We could roll the first strike in the PBA Championship.

Due to our own personal convictions, we probably wouldn't be kicking any ceremonial soccer balls. Again, it's nothing personal to all of you soccer players and soccer moms. It's just our own judgment call.

All in all, we would be the most sports-minded presidents that America has ever seen. We would never wear a business suit onto the ball field. We'd dress appropriately, in baseball, football, or bowling attire. We'll even wear tennis shorts for the US Open.

We're not opposed to showing our knees. If Clinton could show off his knees every time he went jogging, we certainly can do the same with ours. In fact, we might even wear athletic wear all the time around the White House. Although, we understand that after the Clinton administration, Congress passed a law against Spandex.

In closing, if there's one thing that the co-presidency of Rick and Bubba will understand, it will be the world of sports. So bring on that first baseball, that first football, and every other kind of ball (except soccer balls). When we're living at the White House, nothing will ever pre-empt a sporting event. Except maybe World War III. And even that might have to be postponed until after the Super Bowl. That's why we say we need to get more countries involved in America's sports. Then, they'd understand.

FREE TRADE

We believe in free trade. We believe that Rick and Bubba CDs should be available worldwide. We believe our books should be getting into the hands of all the people of the world. We believe that our radio program should be the entertainment on NASA's shuttle flights. As co-presidents of the United States we will do whatever we can to make sure all of this happens and more. This is what makes the concept of free trade make sense to us.

We would like to address some other items, however, that have made the concept of free trade not make sense. Some of what we have been exchanging with our free-trading neighbors should have given us pause. Let's start with all the funny-looking fruit and vegetables that have been showing up at our local grocery stores; things that look like they were left on the shelves by aliens (the spaceship kind of alien, that is).

What is a "kiwano horned melon," and why is it being sold in Alabama? What is dragon fruit? Or blood oranges? Or star fruit? Or plucots? What happened to regular, bloodless oranges, good old-fashioned apples and pears? Did the aliens take those back with them, and leave the weird-looking stuff for us? If so, then maybe there is intelligent life out there.

But we don't think so. And we want our fruit back.

Free trade is fine, but we want our food looking like the food we're used to. Someone's messing with us. Every time you go to the grocery store, there's another strange-looking fruit or vegetable sitting there in a bin. They don't do that with the cereal aisle. Other than an occasional cartoon-driven new cereal, or the addition of some dried fruit inserted into the box, most cereals have pretty much stayed the same. You don't see Frosted Alfalfa Flakes, Shredded Horned Melon, or Trix with Tofu. There's a line of respect there, for both the consumer and the cereal, and it's not crossed.

But the produce aisle has run amok. It has turned into an "anything goes" situation. We'd expect that in California or New York, but this is reaching into the Bible Belt states, and we're fairly sure there's a commandment against it. Maybe not in the Bible itself, but surely in one of the footnotes.

When it comes to other foreign-trade products, this is what we believe. It's good to buy American, but not out of patriotic guilt. You should buy American simply because our products are better. That should be America's goal—to make our products superior and a better value than any of the other guys' products. We should be buying American out of pride and confidence.

I (Rick) never used to buy an American-made car because, frankly, some of the cars that were made in other countries were better. I tried staying with American-made cars, I really did. But I didn't get the same performance from my Ford as I was getting from my Toyota. Sorry. I know this hurts to hear it, it even hurts me to say it, but at one time that really was true. I don't think it's the case anymore. Today, I believe we can hold our own with any car manufacturer in the world. In fact, many of the foreign models are actually made right here in the good ol' USA, which helps provide us with jobs, too.

So now when people say, "Hey, why are you driving a Honda? Why aren't you buying American?" I answer with, *"Hey, it was made in Alabama, you good 'un!"*

Other aspects of free trade have caused us a little concern as well. For instance, can't we come up with some kind of compromise on toys? We're all for cheaper toys, but we don't really want that much lead in our children's diets. These toy recalls of late are costing certain manufacturers millions of dollars. We feel bad for them, but we don't want our kids sucking on a lead pipe disguised as a toy. Maybe next time they'll test and retest the lead content of the products they're ordering before selling it to America's children.

America needs to use more common sense when it comes to the kind of merchandise we're buying from foreign countries. I mean, should China really be supplying our military elite with green berets? Doesn't that seem a little strange to you? Have we forgotten that they're a communist nation and would probably love to do us in? We already gave them intelligence that helped them catch up in their nuclear weapons capabilities and space programs. Now we're letting them dress us, too? It just seems a little ironic to us.

Let's have free trade, but for goodness's sake, let's be smart about it. Besides, how much horned melon can any of us really eat anyway?

TOP TEN REASONS TO ELECT RICK AND BUBBA

10. A Rick and Bubba barbeque might put North Korea's Kim Jong Il in a better mood.

9. Dixie has never designed a set of White House china.

8. More jokes in the State of the Union addresses.

7. We've never had a President Bubba.

6. The White House lawn could use a couple of good hunting towers.

5. Not one, but two fine first ladies.

4. Rick and Bubba need to downsize anyway.

3. It will increase their book sales.

2. If the country has to pay for a presidential limousine, we might as well put two people in there that could fill it.

1. Birmingham could use the break.

~~1, 2, 3, 4~~ 5 GROUPS WHOSE VOTE WE DON'T PLAN ON GETTING

Even though we believe we personify the figurative "everyman" in America, and even though we are approachable, humorous, athletic, and the two best-looking fat men in America, we know that, despite all these admirable qualities, some people will still not vote for us. After dissecting polls and focus groups (and anyone else we had on speed dial), we've determined that the following groups will probably NOT be writing in our names come Election Day:

People who own pit bulls. This is one group that will probably vote for someone else. We don't support pit bulls. Our newspapers are filled with story after story of pit bulls attacking humans. They can be aggressive dogs when provoked. (We realize that Chihuahuas are aggressive dogs, too. But a Chihuahua attack just doesn't carry the same impact as a pit bull attack. One sounds life-threatening, the other sounds embarrassing.)

Pit bulls are in a class by themselves. Being a borderline Libertarian, however, I (Bubba) would stop short of legislative action concerning this.

Anyone who thinks we should have a tax increase. Have you noticed the people who want to raise taxes never want them raised on their own particular tax group? We don't believe in increasing taxes at all. We're taxed enough already. What we do want is all those people who want a tax increase to know that it is perfectly within their right to go ahead and mail in whatever gift they want to the IRS. There is no law on the books prohibiting this. They can include a note that says the extra money is to reduce the deficit, or it's a gift to Uncle Sam, or for the environment—however they want to word it. They are more than welcome to send it in. We're sure the IRS will be happy to accept their donations. They can have as big of a heart as they want when it comes to paying taxes. We just want them to keep their big hearts out of our wallets.

Anybody who tries to outlaw donuts. We don't want the government determining what we can and cannot eat. We want to be able to eat all the cholesterol we want, good or bad. And if jelly-filled donuts contain the occasional trans fat, what concern is that of the government's? (What's good enough for Elvis is good enough for the rest of us.) No one is suggesting that all the joggers and bicyclists start paying an extra road tax because they're using our roads for their exercise program, which, by the way, can possibly cause them to get hit by a car while getting into shape. (This is just one more reason why we don't jog.)

We leave the joggers alone, and we want the government and joggers to leave our relationship with Krispy Kreme alone. Even if it costs us votes.

Whoever decided that police officers have nothing better to do than give seat-belt tickets. No one supports the police, military, and our firefighters more than we do. We have helped them raise money for various causes on more occasions than we can count. We've spoken up for them whenever they've needed someone in their corner.

But this "click it or ticket" campaign that someone came up with is, we believe, a terrible waste of manpower. Why are we using trained professionals who are skilled in weaponry and special tactics to stand out by our public gathering places and hand out seat-belt tickets? Why don't we just let them handle the violent criminals, and let us handle our own self-restraint devices?

Don't get us wrong. We understand the need for seat-belts. They save lives. They really do. But it should be everyone's personal responsibility to see to it that their seat belt is fastened, not the government. Can't we as a nation handle that? What's next, nose-wiping guards?

Because of our stance on this issue, it could cost us some votes. And possibly a ticket or two, on those days when the shoulder strap won't fit over that third trip to the food bar. But we still think we're right.

Soccer families. We don't plan on getting the soccer moms' votes. We're pretty sure they will be casting their ballot for anyone but us. We understand this. But any historian worth his salt would have to agree with us that the ills of our nation have risen in direct correlation with the increase of soccer fields in America. We have no proof, of course, but soccer may have even brought on global warming, if there is such a thing.

MONUMENTAL CHANGES

Do you realize Washington DC has more monuments and statues than any other city in the nation? From the Washington Monument to the Lincoln and Jefferson Memorials, to the statues of Christopher Columbus, Benjamin Franklin, and Albert Einstein, America knows how to honor its most distinguished citizens.

If we are elected co-presidents, we will see to it that the following people are also honored with some sort of statue or memorial:

1. **Willis Haviland Carrier**, the man who invented air conditioning. How can we not pay our respects to this genius? To this day, as far as we know, the "Father of Cool" does not have a statue. Why not? When you consider how hot it can get in the summer here in America, especially in Washington DC, don't you think Willis deserves his own statue? One that stands in, fittingly enough, an air-conditioned building?

2. **Sir John Harrington**, the inventor of the first flushing toilet. He came up with this novel idea back in 1596, and then he proceeded to make one for himself and one for his godmother,

Queen Elizabeth. Where would we be today without Sir John and his invention? I think we would all agree that indoor plumbing has been life changing. Thanks, John, for inventing, well, you know, the john.

3. **John "Big Daddy" Bishop**, owner of Dreamland Barbeque Ribs. For those of you who don't live in the South, trust us on this—Big Daddy deserves a statue. We consider ourselves experts on the subject, and if we have anything to say about it, Big Daddy's ribs will be on the daily menu at the White House. And he will get a statue. Maybe we'll put it next to Big Boy's. Big Daddy and Big Boy. The Rose Garden will never be the same.

4. **Joseph Gayetty**, the man responsible for the first factory-made toilet paper. Thanks to Joe's invention, the use of corncobs and maple leaves became a thing of the past for most of us. Joseph Gayetty invented the paper for the toilet back in 1857. He was so proud of his invention, he had his name printed on every sheet. Of course, those original tributes are long gone. Joe Gayetty deserves a permanent monument.

5. Why isn't there a monument to **Henry Ford** in Washington DC? The invention of the automobile had a huge effect on society. Can you imagine what life would be like if we were all still trying to get around in a horse and buggy? Considering the price of gas, we might have more money in our pockets, but it'd take us two days to get to the supermarket.

6. **Sara Lee**. This is a crime. Since the Sara Lee Bakery first opened its doors back in 1971, no one has suggested a monument to this fine woman. Once in office, we will see to it that this takes place. We might even declare a Sara Lee federal holiday.

7. This may sound self-serving, but we feel there should be a **radio talk show host** memorial. Radio talk show hosts have gotten people thinking, talking, and have been instrumental in making a lot of positive changes in our country. They need their own memorial. Preferably under a canopy of some sort. The open mouths on the statues would be far too inviting to pigeons.

8. There needs to be a memorial to **high school football, basketball, and baseball players** who missed that one important play of their lives. These brave men and women have suffered in silence for long enough; they need to have some place to go to pay homage to their past and other fallen brothers and sisters who missed similar plays and have lost so much of their lives living in regret and shame.

9. We feel there should be a memorial to **political cartoonists and humorists**. Humor plays such an important role in politics, and as far as we know, there is no memorial to the funny men and women who make Washington a little easier to understand.

10. Lastly—and it almost embarrasses us to bring this up (almost, but we'll do it anyway)—we would erect a **Rick and Bubba statue**. We usually shy away from this sort of attention. But if we don't do it, who will? Aside from those in our own homes, we have authorized only a few Rick and Bubba statues in the Birmingham area. But we will make an exception and allow a Rick and Bubba statue to be erected in Washington DC. It wouldn't be taller than the Washington Memorial (we looked into it, and apparently there are ordinances against this). It wouldn't replace any existing memorials, either. Abraham Lincoln looks too comfortable to move him. But before our term is up, I'm sure we'll find a suitable place for our statue.

THE BALCONY VOTE

We're Christians, but we don't wear our denomination on our sleeves. In fact, instead of dividing the candidates by denominations, we feel they should be divided by the truest test of commitment—where they sit in church. In other words, are they balcony or are they main-floor people?

We are both balcony people. Balcony people are closer to God. There is no need for all of you main floor people to get yourself in a huff. It is a simple matter of altitude. When we sing "I'll Fly Away," we don't have as far to go.

Once in a while, main floor people will sit up in the balcony. And vice versa. But the loyalty isn't there. Sometimes a main-floor family will find themselves up in the balcony simply because they arrived late and all the downstairs pews were filled. Balcony people, being the inclusive lot that we are, will welcome them. But we still know they are fish out of water.

When it comes to the music portion of the service, there are major differences between balcony people and main-floor people. Main-floor people are a lot closer to the microphones, so every sour note can be easily picked up. Because of this, main-floor people tend to hold back. But up in the balcony, you can sing to your heart's content. Even if you belt out a note that could shatter plastic, the majority of the congregation won't hear you.

Balcony people also have a better view. We can see who stayed home from church, whose kids are acting up, who's passing the offering plate by without putting anything in it, and who needs Rogaine. You can't do all of that from the main floor. Basically, we're more informed.

The only real downside to being a balcony person is the fact that it's a long way from the altar if you need to go down there and pray. In some churches it's such a hike, you could start heading down there after Sunday morning service, and not reach it until the close of the evening service.

We have tried sitting on the main floor a few times just to see what it's like, but it caused seating pandemonium. Because we had unknowingly taken another family's usual seats, they had to take someone else's usual seats, and they had to take someone else's, and so on, and so on. The pastor could hardly preach that day because his bearing was all thrown off. It did, though, get all those families to church early the next Sunday.

Another measure of the depth of a candidate's faith is how he or she views the importance of the Sunday bulletin. A true person of faith will have a Sunday bulletin in his or her hands at all times during the Sunday morning service. We're not saying the bulletin is as important as the Bible, but we are saying that it is important. If they aren't handing out bulletins at the pearly gates, a few of us Baptists might actually hesitate to go in. We would go in eventually, of course, but we'd complain about the issue to the first usher we ran into.

Bulletins are important because they tell you what's going on during the service and in the coming weeks. Some bulletins even have a tear-off portion where you can register your attendance and write whatever prayer requests you might have. If you don't have a bulletin, it's like you don't have the script. You start squirming and fidgeting and catch yourself looking around to see if anyone has dropped theirs on the ground. You don't care if it's wrinkled and stepped on. You'll just pick it up and pretend it's your own.

When we sit on the main floor, I (Rick) almost always forget to get a bulletin. My whole routine is thrown off. The usher forgets to give me one because I've thrown off his routine, too. But without my bulletin, I feel like a kindergartner on his first day of school. I'm bewildered, overwhelmed, and I just want my mommy.

I will try to get comfort from Sherri, but she usually just wants me to be quiet. She'll even start talking down to me, like I'm one of our kids.

"Rick, can you just keep quiet and listen? You can get a bulletin later."

Of course, that's when I realize that Sherri doesn't have the spiritual depth that I do.

"Sherri, honey, I need my bulletin to write sermon notes," I whisper to her. "Maybe you don't want to write notes about what the pastor is saying, but I do."

Sherri will then point out several of the offering envelopes on which I have drawn a sunshine and a few stick people, and perhaps even a note to her that says, "I love you." She'll think she's making some kind of point, but it's lost on me. All I know is I'm hurt. And bulletin-less.

"I need my bulletin, Sherri."

Some of you may see my bulletin obsession as a negative, but compartmentalizing is a good presidential quality to have. It means that while you're being impeached, you can still keep your mind focused on the day-to-day activities of the White House. So even though Sherri was trying to bring up the offering envelope infraction, I was still able to maintain my focus on the bulletin issue.

Sherri's pretty good at compartmentalizing, too, and is usually able to stay focused on my not needing a bulletin.

"Could you just listen to the sermon, Rick? You don't need a bulletin."

She's wrong, of course. But I realize that she hasn't been a churchgoer for as long as I have. I know the importance of a bulletin. The bulletin informs you of the title of the sermon. It lists all the bullet points and leaves a blank space by each one for your notes. With a bulletin in hand, you know the order of the service, and approximately when the preacher will be closing in on his final point. A bulletin helps you stay focused. Without my bulletin, no matter how hard I try to keep my mind in line, it will start to wander . . .

I wonder what Bubba's doing right now? I wonder where we're going to eat lunch. . . . No, we can't go there. They're always too crowded after church. . . . And I won't get the discount without a bulletin . . . (some restaurants here in the South offer a discount if you can prove you went to church). *I wonder who's going to win the football game today. . . . I wonder if Sherri will wear that cute little . . . wait, and the priest and the rabbi said what? Why is everyone laughing? What was the set up to that punch line? I missed the pastor's whole joke. Where are we at in the sermon notes? Oh, that's right, I DON'T HAVE A BULLETIN!*

Can you feel my pain?

Some churches will put the pastor's bullet points up on the big screen, but it's not the same. I still need paper to write down my personal study notes. And as Sherri already noted, on this day the offering envelope already had my sunshine and stick figures on them.

I have on occasion used the restroom ploy to try to get a bulletin. But Sherri, being the well-experienced mom that she is, will usually catch on and tell me to wait until after the service. Our whispers will sound like a conversation between her and one of the kids.

"I'm going to the restroom. I'll get a bulletin while I'm back there."

"You don't need it."

"Yes, I do."

"No, you don't. Now hush."

"I really need to go bad."

"It can wait."

"No, it can't."

"Stop it."

"Then, can I go get a drink of water?"

"No."

"I'm thirsty."

"You had a drink when we got here."

"That was a long time ago."

"Rick, you're worse than the kids!"

My wife is right about a lot of things, but I happen to know that on this point, she is wrong. I am not any worse than the kids. The kids would have just sat there and kept right on whining through the rest of the service. I, on the other hand, knew how to handle it like an adult. I waited until the pastor had the congregation stand, then I grabbed a bulletin from the pew in front of us. I don't think the couple in front of us minded at all. In fact, the wife turned and smiled at me. Of course, before long I overheard her husband asking, "Where'd our bulletin go?"

"You don't need it."

"Yes, I do."

"No, you don't. Now hush."

"I need to go to the restroom."

"No, you don't."

"Then, can I go get a drink of water?"

"No."

"I'm thirsty."

"You had a drink when we got here."

"That was a long time ago."

"You're worse than the kids!"

A man after my own heart . . . I wonder if he's running for president, too.

THE "LOOK"

Let's be honest—today, in order to get elected president of the United States, you have to have "the look." Most of our former presidents had "the look." John Kennedy, Ronald Reagan, Franklin Delano Roosevelt, and even George Washington with his powdered wig and wooden teeth had it. (Although, now researchers have determined that his teeth were actually made from hippopotamus ivory . . . like it makes a difference.)

A few presidents who didn't have the look did manage to slip through the cracks. Not that they weren't good presidents. They just didn't have the "look."

One who comes to mind is Richard Nixon. The television cameras weren't kind to Tricky Dick. Before the first televised presidential debate in 1960, his opponent, young, tan, and athletic John Kennedy, decided that he wasn't going to be wearing any makeup for the cameras. The elder and far less tanned Nixon decided that he wouldn't wear any television makeup either. That decision, along with a shirt that didn't fit him properly, probably cost him the election. Nixon looked washed out and sick, while Kennedy looked like he had just spent a week at the beach. We understand Nixon was running a fever that night as well. In short, Kennedy had the "look." Nixon didn't, and Nixon lost that election.

Bill Clinton looks presidential, but he also looks like one of your old college buddies, doesn't he? You know, the guy who's the life of a Super Bowl party. It's just hard to place that same guy in the Oval Office. He had the presidential "look," but apparently, not always the presidential behavior.

Gerald Ford had that college buddy look, too. Maybe that's because he used to play football. But he also looked presidential, even when he was falling down stairs. That's not easy to pull off.

Martin Van Buren probably would have looked more presidential without the funny sideburns.

Jimmy Carter looked like a peanut farmer who became president. But then, he was.

Grover Cleveland looked like a man who, like us, moved to the White House just for the two kitchens. He could really put away the groceries, couldn't he? Grover could have held a dual presidency all by himself.

We believe we have the presidential look. Not in our everyday clothes. But when we dress up. We've been told by our wives that we clean up well. We think they meant that as a compliment.

We've also been told that we have a confident manner about us (we don't blink when we order a "triple cheeseburger with fries and supersize the trans fat"). We are clean cut, as opposed to being "cut," which is more of a physique kind of thing. "Clean cut" is more presidential. We can also, on occasion, look rather intelligent. Sometimes the office only requires that you "look" smart, not actually "be" smart. There is a difference. As to which one is more desirable, the jury's still out.

We also walk with a presidential walk. Ronald Reagan had that walk. To be fair, so did Bill Clinton. We can walk like that, too, with our heads raised high and at a confident, determined pace.

We believe voters will agree that we have that "presidential look" and give us a shot at the office come this November. If not, next election we're going with the Martin Van Buren sideburns.

THE MEDICAL
DISCLOSURE

The media and the public seem to want to know everything they can about a candidate's health. They want to make sure that the person on the top of the ticket is going to be around to lead them for four, possibly even eight years. They're usually not all that impressed with the vice-presidential candidate and don't necessarily want him or her running the country. They want their man or woman of choice to be around and executing the duties of president for the entire term.

Since we are running for co-presidents, the health of each one of us is equally important. Let us reassure you the voter that we are in the finest of shape. Despite our almost exclusive diet of trans fats, biscuits and gravy, and red meat, our blood does not have the consistency of motor oil. In fact, recent blood work showed that our cholesterol level was well within the healthy range, give or take a lump or two of cheesecake.

Rick's Medical Disclosure

Once, my blood pressure was so elevated, I was able to enter my initials in the pharmacy self-test blood pressure machine for high score. But with exercise, I've been able to get that down.

Of course, exercise comes with its own risks. I got an elevated diaphragm from jumping on a moonwalk inflatable that was no longer being inflated (the party was shutting down). I went right through it to the pavement. I was lucky to walk away with only the diaphragm injury.

Another medical disclosure concerns my right foot. It has no working ligaments anymore. This is an old football injury that ended my chances of a professional sports career. (Did I mention I used to play a little ball?)

Playing football also left me with a broken nose. My dad set it for me while we were eating dinner that night (we're a close family that way). But it broke again when we were late one day and, after brushing my teeth, I turned to run to the car, but ran smack dab into the door instead. If elected, and until I'm successful in closing down the United Nations, it is very likely that I will speak to them from time to time with tissue stuck up my nose.

Another time I wasn't looking where I was running and ended up cutting off the end of my toe. It happened when I was a child, but to this day it still has not healed properly, mainly due to the fact that my dad (a retired football coach) taped the piece of flesh back on with athletic tape.

Because of all my athletic injuries, my coordination isn't always the best, so Americans should expect me to fall down a lot, much like President Gerald Ford.

Oh yeah—I also have bone fragments floating in my left elbow, a souvenir from horseplay in a parking lot with my friend, Gerald "the Wooly Mammoth" Cates. (Note to self: It's never a good idea to get into a mock wrestling match with someone nicknamed "Wooly Mammoth.")

Other than the above injuries, my last full body MRI showed that all my major organs are operating properly. My kidneys are fine, my heart is operating as it should, my liver is intact, and my lungs are able to handle most flights of stairs. If not, I understand the White House has an elevator.

Now it's Bubba's turn . . .

Bubba's Medical Disclosure

Overall, I am in good shape. My eyesight is going through some changes, though. I used to have the eyesight of an eagle. My optometrist, Dr. David

Chandler, a very good friend now, used to say, "Bubba, if your eyesight was any better, the University of Alabama School of Medicine would do a documentary on you."

But now I'm starting to need glasses. It happened overnight. I don't have bad eyesight. I just need a little help. My doctor told me that I'm just now getting back to where normal eyesight for my age is, and that usually means glasses. I don't mind wearing glasses because a lot of people think they make you look more presidential.

Another medical disclosure that I need to make is something that I already talked about in one of our previous books. I tend to overindulge at Thanksgiving. In fact, I once had to have my stomach pumped because I had eaten too much. I'm not proud of this, and I've worked through the matter in therapy. But I do need to be forthright about the incident.

As your president, I will try to not overeat on special occasions, but as we've already made perfectly clear, we make no promises.

COMPLETING THE SMITHSONIAN

One great thing about living in Washington is that you get to visit the Smithsonian whenever you want. The Smithsonian has just about everything you can think of—from the Wright Brothers' airplane, to the wooden lap desk on which Thomas Jefferson wrote the Declaration of Independence.

There are a few national treasures of historic importance that the Smithsonian doesn't have yet. Once elected, we will see to it that the process of locating the following items and acquiring them for the museum begins right away.

Here is what we would like to see added:

★ The birdshot removed from Dick Cheney's hunting partner.

★ Old gas station sign inscribed with the price of $0.49 a gallon and "a free drinking glass with fill up."

★ The Rick and Bubba Fun-Mobile. As already mentioned, this was my (Rick) personal van that we covered in Rick and Bubba handwritten ads. It was the only advertisement we could afford, and I drove it all around town. But only in a forward direction. (Remember: The car had no reverse gear so I had no choice other than to go forward.)

★ Bubba's crown from being crowned Homecoming King back in 1982. (If elected, he will only wear this crown on special occasions. Like when the Queen of England is visiting.)

★ Rick's football jersey. There is no debating that ol' 75 deserves to be in the Smithsonian. I (Rick) don't know if all of you readers know this (I've barely mentioned it five or six times in our books), but I played a little ball in my day. I was a pretty big guy even back then, so football was a natural choice for me. If they can't give my old jersey its own display case, maybe they could use it for a curtain.

★ A pair of MC Hammer pants. Without solid proof, future generations might not believe it.

★ Bubba's baseball glove from the season that he should have won a baseball state championship. He was robbed of the award because of an alleged illegal player. Placing his glove in the Smithsonian should help ease some of the pain. That and a few more years of scream therapy.

★ The microphones used on the very first Rick and Bubba Show back in 1994. We could auction these off on eBay, but figure we owe it to the country to make them available for all our citizens to view.

★ Bubba's car stereo from his 280z in the 1980s. He has since sold the car, but he should have held onto that stereo. It was ahead of its time.

★ The General Lee. 'Nuff said.

We'll probably come up with a few more items by the time we get to the White House. But this is a good starting point.

KEEPING YOUR EYES
ON THE PRIZE

Jimmy Carter has one. Woodrow Wilson and Teddy Roosevelt have one apiece. And now, even Al Gore has one. We want ours, too.

What are we talking about? The Nobel Peace Prize, of course. Apparently, politicians have a good shot at winning this coveted award, and once in office we are going to do everything in our power to acquire one of those babies ourselves (no disrespect intended).

Frankly, we think it would be a hoot to win the Nobel Peace Prize. Since they still haven't retired our sports jerseys from our high schools, winning this award would be a close second. We understand a substantial check even comes with the award. It's like winning the Publisher's Clearing House Sweepstakes, only in Oslo.

We're already trying to figure out what we have to do to give ourselves the best shot at a Nobel Peace Prize. Al Gore wrote a book and a documentary about global warming. We could have done that. But it's just been so doggone hot lately.

Jimmy Carter helped broker a truce in the Middle East, which seemed to give him an edge in the contest. We could send in the National Guard to *The View*, but we don't know if that's enough to get the attention of the Nobel Prize committee.

Keeping your eyes on the prize isn't always easy. There are so many distractions. I think it's the word *peace* in the title that throws you off. Promoting peace doesn't usually get a lot of attention.

Since both of us have kids, we're well practiced in keeping the peace. Marriage gives you experience with this as well. If we're elected, it will be the first time we've had to keep the peace globally, but how different could it be? Dealing with a rogue nation has got to be similar to dealing with an unruly teenager.

"We need to talk."

"About what?"

"You invaded another country."

"Who snitched?"

"It doesn't matter who snitched. You did it. Now say you're sorry."

"I don't want to."

"Do it anyway."

"They started it."

"Well, you can stop it."

"You always side with them."

"I'm siding with what's right. You invaded their space."

"So?"

"You can't do that."

"Oh, brother . . ."

"Don't you roll your eyes at me!"

"Who's gonna stop me?"

"That does it! Get back into your own country and don't come out until you can behave yourself!"

Teddy Roosevelt won a Nobel Peace Prize, and it's probably because of all the experience he got in peace-keeping with all his kids. Having lots of kids pays off in both wisdom and in knowing the right words to say for any situation, including foreign affairs.

Like Teddy, we have lots of kids, and although we don't want to sound presumptuous, we've already cleared a space on our wall for the award.

Peace out.

THE NEW LIST OF "ENDANGERED" RESOURCES

As presidential candidates we're quite aware that many resources are diminishing and are even endangered today. But in our presidency, we want to broaden the focus of endangered resources. We want to look beyond wetlands, habitat, fossil fuels, and various species of wood rats. There are some important resources we feel are diminishing more quickly than sub-prime loans.

For example, whatever happened to common sense? Sense that tells you not to balance a scalding cup of McDonald's coffee between your legs while you're driving. Sense that tells you an all-you-can-eat buffet doesn't really have to be all you can eat. Sense that tells you you're not going to win a high-speed Los Angeles car chase when every news and police helicopter is following you.

Years ago, people seemed to have a lot more common sense. Your mom and dad, your school, and your church made sure they instilled plenty of it in you because they knew you'd need it in life. Today, books on dumb crooks, celebrity bloopers, embarrassing moments, stupid insurance claims, and ridiculous court cases are in their fourth and fifth volumes. If there is any common sense left on the planet, a lot of us don't seem to be using it. Common sense is number one on the Rick and Bubba Endangered List.

Patience is another endangered quality. One short drive down any downtown street in America during rush hour will prove this. People ride your tail, cut you off, and display all kinds of interesting hand signals (and they aren't telling you they're making a left turn, either).

Kindness is becoming endangered, too. Have you noticed that people seem a lot meaner than they used to be? Comedy has gotten meaner too. Even clowns are painting on a permanent snarl.

Contentment is quickly becoming a casualty, too. People today are augmenting this body part, lipo-suctioning that, all in an effort to feel good about themselves. They're getting tucked, sucked, and plucked and still hate their faces and thighs.

Grace and mercy are two other resources on the endangered list. If you don't believe us, analyze your reaction to the latest celebrity scandal or personal failure of someone you know. Did you reach out to help, maybe say a sincere prayer for that person, or were you laughing at the latest version of the story on YouTube and texting your friends with witty criticisms? (That poor Miss Teen USA girl comes to mind—you know, the one who thinks we don't have enough maps in "those Asian countries and the Iraq." How many laughs did everyone have at her expense? But she was right. Maps really are a good thing. Who can argue with that?)

Another endangered quality today is communication. It's ironic that with all our cell phones, text messaging, and BlackBerries, we rarely sit down and really talk to each other any more (*ttyl* and *lol* don't count). How many of us know our neighbors as well as we know *The Office* cast? How many of our kids learn more from SpongeBob or Hannah Montana than from us? Wives and husbands misunderstand each other all the way to the divorce court. Bosses and employees don't communicate. These days, it's easier to sign-on to a computer for information than to tune-in to those you care about.

Okay, so we're on a soap box. Or a stump. Or whatever presidential candidates stand on to talk. But before we get down, there's one more pair of vanishing resources that saddens us: innocence and decency. Just turn on your television set and you'll understand. We've gone from *Little House on the Prairie* and *The Cosby Show* to *Dirty, Sexy, Money* and *Desperate Housewives*.

If elected, we pledge to do whatever we can to bring back some of these valuable endangered resources. We are firm believers in the "It's never too late" philosophy. Just look at our candidacy (or in our closets) and you'll know that.

WHAT'S RIGHT
ABOUT AMERICA

At a time when so much of what we're hearing has to do with what's wrong with America, we want to take this opportunity to point out what's right about this great land of ours.

1. *Our Football*

One thing that's right about America is our football. When you look around at the rest of the world, you see that a lot of other countries don't play football, not our kind of football, anyway. They play ball with their feet, but that's soccer. Granted, some call it *futbol*, but that's spelled funny. We play football, and we have the courage to spell it and call it that, even though the ball actually gets kicked by only one or two guys on the team. We're just that bold. We can look the people of the world in the eye and say, *"It is too football! Now get over it!"*

If you ask us, the world would be a much safer place if more countries played American football. Soccer is such a low scoring game, no wonder so many of its fans get so cranky. It's hard to sit there and watch the scoreboard hour after hour with nothing much happening. Also, in soccer you're not allowed to use your hands to touch the ball. That's got to lead to some suppressed anger issues, don't you think?

It is for this reason that we feel we as Americans should work harder to export more of our sports around the world. If we could get terrorists and suicide bombers to do the wave instead of strapping explosives to themselves, wouldn't the world be a much better place?

2. *Our Military*

Our military is another thing that's right about America. You won't find a more dedicated, selfless, brave, and skilled military than ours. Have there been a few bad apples in the bunch? Sure. But thankfully, they're the exception to the rule.

Not only is our military the best in the world, but they don't do that weird high step march that some other militaries do. (Have you noticed that whenever a military does that high step march, they're usually planning to take over the world?)

We have no intention of taking over the world, and so we don't do the high step. Our march is much cooler than that. We move in formation, but we're not trying to kick the helmet off the guy in front of us with every step.

3. *Our Food*

Another thing that's right about America is our food. We've got so much, we're feeding a lot of the world from our abundance. We may very well be the present-day land of milk and honey. There's so much food in America, even our vegetables are getting jobs in the movies.

We have our share of poor, but even our poor don't look so poor when you compare them to other countries. Sorry, but if you're wearing a leather team jacket and living in the box your big screen television set came in, all the while approaching strangers on the street saying, "Brother, can you spare an iTunes gift card," you're probably not truly poor. You've got it better than a lot of people in the world, so be thankful.

4. *Our Flag*

Our flag is one more thing that's right about America. In our opinion America's flag is a lot cooler than most other flags, with the possible exception of Great Britain. Great Britain has our same colors, and we like all those crosses and lines. We like how the cross is dominant over the "x" and not the other way around. It's just cool. Like our flag is cool.

We're sorry to say, and this is just our opinion, but the design on Canada's flag isn't one of our favorites. It's nothing personal against our Canadian friends, and no disrespect of their flag is intended, but leafs aren't very intimidating. Canada can have a leaf if they want, but we're glad America went with stars and stripes.

As far as threatening images go, the Canadian leaf is at least better than what is on Norfolk Island's flag. They've got a Christmas tree on theirs. It's a nice tree, but it brings to mind candy canes, mistletoe, and a fat man whose belly shakes like a bowl full of jelly—not exactly a force to be reckoned with.

Antarctica has a flag that doubles as a map. That's actually a good idea. That way if their troops ever get lost, they just get the guy in the front of the line carrying the flag to stop, and they can check out their location. It's sort of like MapQuest on a stick. Miss Teen USA would be thrilled.

We like our flag best. We're sure the citizens of Canada and Antartica like their flags, too. But this is our book. We get to talk about how much we love our flag. A lot of people have died for it. Our flag can look both comforting and powerful when it waves in the middle of a battle, national disasters, political rallies, and school assemblies. It can make your chest swell with pride and your eyes tear up with thankfulness. It's a cool flag (or Grand Ole' flag, for you purists).

5. *Our Tunes*

America has great music, too. From Elvis to Johnny Cash, from Bruce Springsteen to Ray Charles to Barbra Streisand, and countless others, America doesn't take a musical backseat to anyone. Even the so-called British musical invasion had a lot of America's blues and rock and roll influences. When it comes to music, we have the best. Has anything from around the world even come close to *Sweet Home Alabama?* We rest our case.

6. *Our Parties*

America can put on a celebration like nowhere else in the world. We may not have coronations, but we sure know how to party. We love fireworks. We'll shoot them off for just about any occasion. Fourth of July? Fireworks. New Year's Eve? Fireworks. Super Bowl? Fireworks. Homerun at the local minor league baseball team? Fireworks. Spending your kids' inheritance on your vacation? Fireworks. We love to celebrate, and we believe we do it better than anyone else.

7. *Our Sporting Events*

We even do sporting events like no other country. Compare our Super Bowl to the World Cup. The World Cup is a big event, but how many companies are lining up to pay two and a half million dollars for thirty seconds of commercial time on it? Has Aerosmith ever played during halftime at a soccer championship? The Super Bowl will have six concerts before kickoff. And that's not counting all the dancing the players do after a touchdown. And where in the world does anything compare to the intensity (or the bracket pools) of March Madness? No, the running of the bulls doesn't come close, and neither does the World Curling Federation Championships. The USA knows how to do sports.

8. *Our National Anthem*

Another thing that's right about America is our national anthem. Our anthem has been sung by the greatest singers (outside of Roseanne Barr) of our time—Barbra Streisand, Whitney Houston, Sandy Patti, Lee Greenwood, Gloria Estefan, and Elvis.

Even Canadian Celine Dion has sung it for us. Can you imagine Whitney Houston (the pre-Bobby Brown Whitney) singing *Oh, Canada*? Again, it's nothing against our northern neighbors (we're sure they love their national anthem, too), but you just don't hear about a lot of American celebrities lining up to sing about that leaf. And excuse our asking, but do they even have flyovers during the singing of *Oh, Canada*? Flyovers are big here in America. We will fly a live eagle in over people's heads and land him at the fifty-yard line if we think we can get a good reaction for the camera. That's primarily what the fireworks are for. And the flyovers. We love scaring the daylights out of people. That's why heart attacks are our number one killer. They tell us it's because of our diet. It's not. It's our surprise flyovers.

9. *Freedom of Speech*

Our freedom of speech is definitely another thing that's right about America. Where else can you appear on television, radio, or in print and say that the president is goofy and make fun of him or her as much as you want and nobody comes and carries you off to jail? Or worse yet, disengages your tongue from your body. Obviously, we can't yell "Fire!" in a crowded building unless it is, in fact, on fire. But we have a lot of liberty to express our opinions here in this country. Do they have that same freedom in, say, Venezuela?

The bottom line is there is a lot more that's right about America than what's wrong. It's easy for others to take a swipe at the prosperity of America, but where else can a person who was born into poverty raise his or her standard of living to millionaire status? (And where else can you become a millionaire in one night on television shows like *Deal or No Deal*?)

It's easy for others to take a swipe at the politics of America, but any natural born citizen has a chance to run for president of our great country. Immigrants can even start their careers off as bodybuilders, develop into major movie stars, and then decide they want to be governor of the most populated (and hummus-eating) state in the land. And still keep their accent. (We love you, Ah-nuld.)

And we as citizens can let our voices be heard Election Day, although sadly, it seems like more people let their voices be heard on *American Idol* than at the polls.

It's easy for others to take a swipe at the freedom of religion of this nation. But as we said before, our freedom *of* religion was never intended to keep us *from* religion. The majority of us realize that it is our faith in God that has played the biggest role in making this country great.

It's easy for others to point to division in our country. But there is far more that unites us, than divides us. Take Starbucks, for example.

It's easy for others to take advantage of our goodness, to call on us when they're in trouble, only to turn their backs on us when we ask for their help in return. We continue to do good anyway.

It's easy for others to say that we take our blessings for granted. There, they may have a point. Too often we do.

Are there areas where America can improve? Of course there are. By working together, we can make our country even greater. We may not agree on everything, but if we can all agree on enough to keep America moving forward, then our future is in good hands. The people's hands.

Now how's that for sounding presidential? At the very least, co-presidential?

Rick and Bubba's Recommendations for New Federal Holidays

For a long time now (probably since kindergarten), we have felt that there weren't enough federal holidays on the calendar. If elected, we are going to do something about this national travesty. We would like to propose that the following be officially added to the nation's roster of federal holidays:

National Spam Day. It is no longer politically correct to make fun of Spam. Despite all the jokes, Spam is still a meat and is entitled to all the privileges and respect that other meats get. Who among us has not had a fried Spam sandwich at sometime throughout his or her life and actually enjoyed it? So why the pretension? We all know with enough ketchup it's pretty tasty. It deserves its own day.

National Free Parking Day. This is a day when you can park anywhere you want. You are free to ignore all the "No Parking" signs and just leave your car wherever you please. If you have to go to the mall, this would be a good day to do it.

National "Hunting with the Guys" Day. Why should husbands have to go through all the begging and doing extra chores around the house just to get out for a day of hunting? Let's make a federal holiday for this and bring back a little peace on earth.

National "Mom's Time Out" Day. In the interest of fairness (and so Dad's hunting day will easily sail through Congress), we will push for a Mom's Time Out Day, too. She will be free to do whatever she wants. (And Dad can line up a babysitter for the kids and go hunting again.)

National Husband/Wife Forgiveness Day. The Jewish religion has a Day of Atonement, but we could use something like this on a national level to help slow down the rising rate of divorce. This would be a day where couples are required to wipe the marriage slate clean of any past infractions and start all over again. No carryovers would be allowed. Hurt feelings from twenty years ago have to be forgiven and forgotten. Some husbands and wives have such a difficult time forgiving, saying "I'm sorry," or accepting responsibility for their own actions, they need the whole day off to prepare for it.

National Cheap Gas Day. This would be a day when gas stations would be federally mandated to lower their gas prices per gallon to somewhere under the price of a two bedroom home. This would be a special day where we could all fill up our tanks at, say $1.20 a gallon, and be able to use the extra money to eat again.

National Super Dad's Day. We realize we already have Father's Day. But this is a special day set aside for all those Super Dads who really step up to the plate and go above and beyond the call of duty. A Super Dad won't just buy his son a skateboard. He'll go skateboarding with him. He won't just send him off to bed. He'll sit there and read to him. He'll take him to baseball practice and maybe even coach the team. Super Dads are always ready to listen, and they aren't afraid to admit when they're wrong. Super Dads need their own day.

National Super Mom's Day. You can usually tell which moms are Super Moms by the bags under their eyes. These are the moms who have carpooled more than their fair share, taken treats to the school because another parent forgot it was his day to bring them, picked up a carload of kids from the bus after camp so that those kids' parents wouldn't have to get out in the rain, and have on more than one occasion had an entire Girl Scout Troop in their home for a sleep-over. And somehow they can still put together a coherent sentence the following morning. They need their own day.

National Common Sense Day. This would be a day where all government officials, all school teachers and administrators, all workers everywhere, and teenagers and children have to use common sense. All decisions made on this day have to be made based solely on good old-fashioned common sense. When you think about it, it could change life as we know it.

VICTORY SPEECH FOR WHEN ALL MAJOR NETWORKS CALL THE RACE IN OUR FAVOR

Load up the U-Haul, Momma! We're going to Washington! We can't believe it either! After months and months of hard work, a Rick and Bubba co-presidency is finally a reality!

We'd like to give a shout out to all the millions of people who took the time to write our names on their ballots. We realize the polls out West and those in the central and eastern time zones still haven't closed yet, but with a total of twelve absentee ballots counted so far, every major network is declaring us the winner!

There are so many people that we would like to thank, we hardly know where to begin. Okay, let's begin with us. As you know, we both worked hard getting our message out to the people. We had to attend countless dinners, luncheons, town hall meetings, and potlucks. It was grueling! There were times when we could hardly lift our forks to our mouths. Somehow we found the strength within us to do it, but it wasn't easy.

We also had to debate our fellow contestants—uh, we mean candidates. We had to track them down in their dressing rooms before the real debates, and try to get them to answer a few questions with us. They never seemed to have enough time to listen to our rebuttals, what with security whisking us off in such a hurry, but we let them (and all the viewers of the evening newscasts) know where we stood on the issues, and it has paid off.

We couldn't have done it without each and every one of you who took the time to make thousands of annoying calls to voters during their dinner hour, who wore your "Elect Rick and Bubba" T-shirts every day to work and around town, who bought our books to send to your friends and relatives, and who ran out at all hours of the night to get our take-out orders. It is because of your commitment to our cause (and the networks' usual rush to scoop the election) that we are now able to declare this win before the majority of the country has even voted. We are and will forever be indebted to you.

See you at the meat-and-three in Washington!

SPEECH FOR WHEN NETWORKS WITHDRAW THEIR PREMATURE ANNOUNCEMENT OF OUR VICTORY

We are saddened to have to announce that the announcement of our landslide victory should never have been announced in the first place. Apparently, it wasn't a land slide. Not that much land slid at all. The networks jumped the gun when they declared us the winner. With only twelve votes counted (absentee ballots from our own district), they thought they were seeing a trend and could give a credible prediction of our win. They have since determined that the race is still too close to call.

In light of this embarrassing situation, all three networks have just now released the following joint announcement:

"We sincerely regret calling the presidential election as early as we did. We failed to realize that it was only noon in California. And that it was still October. We have since rescinded our prediction of a Rick and Bubba win, and will do what we should have done in the first place and wait for the entire nation's polls to close before calling the election for any candidate. We apologize for any inconvenience or embarrassment this may have caused to the Rick and Bubba camp, and we sincerely hope that they haven't already eaten through their victory party's refreshments."

It was a nice apology, but it places us in an awkward position. If we go ahead and cancel the moving truck, and then end up winning after all, how will we get all of our stuff to Washington? Does the presidential limousine even *have* a luggage rack?

On the other hand, if we don't cancel the moving truck, and end up not needing it, we may not be able to get our deposit back. Do you see our quandary here?

If you ask us, a presidential election should be like a game of checkers. You know how if you take your fingers off the game piece, the move still counts? We say if the networks prematurely announce a winner, they shouldn't be allowed to take it back even if their prediction is incorrect. That should be it. No take-backs. It's not fair to the American people or the candidate, and it would teach the networks a lesson once and for all.

Of course, there is the risk of a network going ahead and declaring its favorite candidate the winner, just to manipulate the outcome of the election. But come on, would a network really stoop to doing something that partisan and underhanded?

Okay, let us rephrase that.

What we're saying is this—we don't think it's fair to get a candidate's hopes up, to wake him up from his election night nap and make him get out of his pajamas, throw on a suit, grab his acceptance speech, drive through Sonic for a bite to eat, and then head on down to his waiting supporters, only to have the whole thing taken away from him before the applause even dies down.

But until this practice is corrected, we will have to abide by the election rules and accept the rescinding of the networks' premature announcement of our win. At least until all the votes are tallied, and then, we will once and for all be declared the official winners. And yes, they will have to order more refreshments.

CONCESSION SPEECH FOR WHEN THE VOTES ARE FINALLY COUNTED AND WE'VE BEEN FOUND WANTING

Some people might consider this a concession speech. We do not. We are simply announcing that due to the fact that someone else will be living in the White House for the next four years, we will no longer be seeking the co-presidency of the United States.

Moving there at this point would be considered sour grapes.

It was a hard-fought campaign. We gave it our all. Our supporters did, too. Historically, election night has been a night for taking the high road, for not whining, for not crying over spilt milk.

We'd like to change all of that.

It isn't fair! We should have won! We are calling for a recount! We happen to know for a fact that we received more than twenty votes! By our calculations, at the very least we should have had received the following:

Sherri	One vote
Betty	One vote
Bubba's mom	One vote
Rick's parents	Two votes
Sherri's parents	Two votes
Betty's parents	Two votes
Staff at radio station	Five votes minimum
Pastors	Two votes
Rick and Bubba fans	Four million (give or take four million)

Even if our wives and parents didn't vote for us, we still had our staff and all our Rick and Bubba fans. We know Speedy, Don Juan, and the others would have voted for us, because their Christmas bonuses hung in the balance. Our fans are some of the most loyal fans in all of radio. They would have voted for us, too. So you can understand our skepticism over the fairness of the election, can't you? The numbers just don't add up.

There is an even bigger story here. We just don't know what it is yet. But once we find it, we'll take this all the way to the Supreme Court if necessary. (By the way, we didn't really mean those remarks about the Supreme Court justices being old and wearing their robes everywhere. They're a fine group of the best legal minds in the nation, and we know they'll rule fairly in this situation.)

Until this matter is resolved, we are not conceding this race! We are not throwing in the towel! We are not giving up! We had our tuxes pressed for the Inaugural Ball. The U-Haul's packed and ready to go. We've already notified our paperboy to hold off throwing the newspapers up on our roof for the next four years. Our mail is being held at the post office. There's only one thing for us to do now—America, start the recount!

CONCESSION SPEECH FOR WHEN THE FOURTH AND FINAL RECOUNT HAS BEEN PERFORMED AND EVERY HANGING CHAD HAS BEEN ACCOUNTED FOR . . . AND ONCE AGAIN WE'VE BEEN FOUND WANTING

We received word today that every single last hanging chad has been accounted for and the vote is now official—the Rick and Bubba write-in ticket has lost the election. We do not blame anyone for this unfortunate turn of events. The people have spoken. Incorrectly, but they have spoken. We have no choice but to accept their wishes, no matter how uninformed, naive, and mistaken they are.

We have even forgiven our wives for not voting for us. Betty and Sherri did not really want to move to Washington DC, and so their actions are understandable. We could have used their votes, but we still love them.

We sincerely apologize to the rightful winner for making this election drag on two years into the new term. We tried our best to hurry the recount process along, but we had to do so much of the recounting ourselves, and it took more time than we realized. We did, however, enjoy visiting all the different voting districts throughout our nation and getting to know so many of you fine Americans, not to mention all those sharp lawyers we encountered. We knew all those "Give It Up, Rick and Bubba!" and "Admit It! You Lost, Losers!" signs that many of you were carrying were simply your secret code of encouragement to us. Since the winner had been sworn in and was already serving as your president, you didn't want to seem unsupportive of the new administration. The only way you could let us know that you were standing with us was through these subliminal messages on your picket signs. We got your message loud and clear.

It is unfortunate that the Supreme Court also seemed to drag its robes when it came to making a decision in this case. Their vote kept coming down against us, and so we had to keep filing the case again. Each time they would give us some speech about their last ruling being the final say in the matter, but that only slowed down the process even more. They really should get their act together over there and quit being so stubborn. But that's a battle for another day.

We want to thank all of our supporters for showing up today in the parking lot of Kroger's for our long-awaited concession speech. You are a faithful throng . . . group . . . okay, handful, who realize the importance of the issues that we have raised during this campaign. We wish more reporters had showed up today, but we do want to thank those of you who are here—*Weekly World News* and the student reporters from our kids' schools. Apparently, the other media outlets, as well as the nation as a whole, have moved on with their lives and accepted the outcome of the election.

We must now do the same.

But it's still not fair!

WHEN ALL IS SAID AND DONE

At some time during the night of every Election Day, someone is declared the winner. All of America wakes up knowing who the next president and vice-president are going to be.

We've shared a lot of our dreams, our concerns, and our hopes for America during this campaign. Whether you've agreed with every point we've raised or not, we hope the journey has been fun. We feel better because we've been able to get a lot of things off our chest. And thanks to the meals on the campaign circuit, we've also been able to get a lot of things into our stomachs.

Every four years Americans get to voice their opinions on what's wrong, what's right, and what can be improved upon in our great country. Outsiders looking in must stand in awe that we can get away with saying some of the things we Americans say about our leadership. They must marvel at our freedom of the press. We are a lucky lot. We openly debate our differences, but always seem to be able to pull together in the bad times. Even when we disagree, and sometimes we disagree strongly, over issues facing our nation, there is still a sense of pride that wells up within each one of us whenever we hear our national anthem. We're family.

The White House is our house. One leader gets to live there at a time, but it belongs to all of us. You can visit it any time you want. There are visiting hours, of course (everyone likes to know when company's coming), but generally speaking, the White House is open to us all.

Congress is our family, too. They don't operate in a vacuum. They're there because we've sent them there. It is their job to represent us. If they ever fail to do that, we can call them up, or e-mail them. We can change horses the next time around. We don't have to hold our noses and vote. We can vote in the man or woman we feel best represents our interests. We can even visit Congress and see them in session. Drop in some time. You might come away with a new appreciation for how our country works.

The Supreme Court is family, too, even if they dress a little funny. All families have a few of those, right? The Supreme Court isn't really elected (sort of like in-laws that you don't always get a choice about either, but you learn to adapt). We have no doubt that the justices love America, and are trying to do their best to protect our Constitution. After over two hundred years, we'd have to say that overall, they've done a good job.

The IRS is even family—sort of like that brother-in-law who is always asking for money. But even the IRS has to operate under the rules of the family. If they are getting too powerful, the family has a right to take the brother-in-law aside and remind him of his place.

America is a government of the people, by the people, and for the people. Along the way, some of us have lost sight of that. Instead of communicating with each other and improving things, we've handed over our responsibility to the handful of relatives who do show up every four years to voice their opinions and vote for the new family spokesperson.

That barely half of us show up to vote in an election is a slap in the face of every man and woman who has given up their life for that freedom. Some give the excuse that they don't feel their vote counts. Let us assure you that it absolutely does. In fact, it counts the most inside your own heart, knowing that whoever is in office got there because the majority of Americans wanted him or her there. When all of us don't vote, it leaves us with questions of what might have been if so many Americans had taken the time to get informed and voice our opinion.

Whichever way the election goes this time, we hope that we can all sit back and say to ourselves that we did our part in deciding the future direction of our country. Be an active voter. Investigate a politician's standing on the issues you care most about, not just his (or her) hairstyle or political party. Know why you're voting for that particular candidate. You'll need to remind yourself of that when those elected make their first mistake in office. And they will. Just like you make mistakes at your job, too.

We've said it throughout this book, and we'll close by saying it again. We love America. There is no other country like her on earth. We are blessed to have been born here. No wonder so many people are trying to get here in any way they can. This is the land of opportunity. The rest of the world covets our freedoms.

If we have a flaw, it's our own lack of appreciation that we sometimes show for our blessings. We take an awful lot for granted. It's easy to complain about the things we wish were different. But when you compare our problems with those of other people around the world, we're pretty well off.

We hope we've made you laugh, and maybe even think, but most of all we hope we've reminded you of America's greatness. Just like a family, sometimes we need to remember the value of what we have before we lose it.

See you at the polls!

EPILOGUE:
FROM A FATHER'S HEART

On January 22, 2008, I was given the opportunity to speak from a father's heart to those gathered at the memorial service of my youngest son, William Bronner Burgess. It was an opportunity that most of us wish we are never given, and I only say "opportunity" because of what has taken place in the aftermath of that service.

Before I go on, I first want to say that the prayers, love, and support that we have been shown by so many of you have overwhelmed our family. But it has not surprised us. The Bible says that the world will know us by our love for each other, and we have been showered with that love. We appreciate it so much.

On January 19th, I was speaking at a youth conference in Tennessee with my good friend Scott Dawson when I received the news of Bronner's death, the most horrible news a father could ever receive. Immediately the verse John 16:33 came to mind. In that Scripture Jesus said, "In this world you will have trouble." You see, we live in a fallen world. He never promised us that our lives would be easy. In fact, do you know that in the scriptures Jesus speaks to trials and tribulations far more than He speaks about good times? But He also said, "But take heart, because I have overcome the world."

I remember when my wife Sherri came up with the name Bronner. I thought to myself, "*Bronner*" *sounds like somebody's last name.* I had selected another "B" name (all of our children have "B" names), but we decided to go with Sherri's choice, Bronner. I realize now that Bronner was the perfect name because it's so memorable. Every day countless letters, phone calls, and e-mails continue to come into our office sharing how people are coming to faith through the testimony of William Bronner Burgess. That's amazing when you consider that 90 percent of believers have never shared the gospel with anyone. If the death of our son has been the catalyst for all of us to get our spiritual lives in order and to start going about the Great Commission, then it was not in vain. I would like nothing more than for our loss to energize all believers to start thinking in terms of eternity and what's most important in life. Quit trying to be defined by what you do at work, or what you accomplish in your hobbies. Quit trying to have your children be defined by how good they do in Little League, or in the classroom, or feeling defeated when they fall short. Be defined as a father and a mother by how godly and powerful your children are as warriors for the kingdom of God, and by how they can get up after a failure, or two or three, and get back into the fight.

The stuff of this world means nothing. It is fading away. A few days after Bronner's death I walked into my office where he would always go and play, where no matter how many times I told him not to, he would dump crayons out right on the new carpet. I walked in there after he was gone and saw all his crayons lying on the floor right where he had left them. I took my foot and stepped right on them and ground them into the carpet. Who cares about crayons on the carpet? *WHO CARES?* I might leave that stain on that carpet forever to remind me that it's *just a stupid carpet.*

Some people have asked "Why would God allow Bronner to be taken?" Some people will bring God's love into question because of this. But God's love for us is never in question. You see, we were all doomed to eternal judgment. God is a holy God and even the best of us don't measure up. But God looked at us, and the gulf of sin between Him and us, and because He is a loving God He said, "They can't come to me. I will go to them." So He took on flesh, was born of a virgin, and He walked this earth, feeling everything we feel. He was 100 percent man and 100 percent God. God needed atonement for the sins of man, and He allowed His Son Jesus to suffer a gruesome, humiliating death in our place. Jesus died on that cross for you and me, and, this is the most amazing part, *when He didn't have to.* Some of us walk around like we had that sacrifice coming. *We didn't have that coming! We don't deserve it.* We had hell coming but He died for us anyway. And then he defeated death and He walked out of the tomb on the third day to complete the job. He ascended to heaven, and now He is preparing a place for us to come and join Him for eternity.

I know my son Bronner is there with Him right now because the Bible tells me that he is. Bronner, or "Cornbread," which is what we called him, is with the only Father who loves him more than me. I don't believe for a moment that God took our son away from us to hurt us, or to punish us, or to bring us heartache and pain. But He did allow him to be taken at this time, and there is a plan in it.

As I was flying home that night to be with Sherri and the rest of the family, after having just received the worst news a father could ever receive, I looked out that airplane window at the stars and asked, "Hey, what are You doing, Father? Savior? What are you trying to teach me? This is a hard lesson."

But in Psalm 139 the Bible says that "all our days are numbered." Bronner's death didn't take Him by surprise. I believe God allowed our son to be taken so that His name could be glorified.

God has our family in His hands. He did that day when He took Bronner home, and He did the day He gave me a godly woman as a wife. Sherri Burgess stepped up in my life when no one else would. We took each other's hands on the day we were married, the holiest day of our lives, and we knew that God had a plan for us. I believe this godly wife and outstanding, godly mother will have a huge impact on the kingdom through what she's done as my helper and what she's done for our children and what she was doing as Bronner's mother.

As parents, Sherri and I can think of no greater reward than to one day stand before our Savior in heaven and watch each one of our children, beginning with the first family evangelist, William Bronner Burgess, receive a "Well done, good and faithful servant." That's a parent's highest calling. A friend's highest calling. It's the calling of every believer.

If you're reading this today and you are not 100 percent sure of where you're going to spend eternity, I want you to know that you can be sure. In John 14:6, Jesus said, "I am the way, the truth, and the life. No one comes to the

Father except through Me." I didn't say it. Jesus did. The Bible also says in John 14:1, "Let not your heart be troubled; you believe in God, believe also in Me."

My desire is that the death of my son will bring many to a place of faith in Jesus Christ. We also pray it will energize Christians to be serious about their faith and about sharing the gospel with those around them. It's already started. If you don't know Jesus Christ, nothing would thrill Sherri and me more than for you to honor my son's memory by accepting Jesus as your Savior. If you do, please write to us and let us know.

Thank you for allowing me to share my heart with you. Whoever wins the presidency, as important as that is, it's not nearly as important as where you spend eternity.

In closing, the Burgess family wants to give all honor and glory to God for the many blessings He has given us, especially for the life of Bronner Burgess. And while we do not understand, we know Who is in charge and that His will be done in life and in death.

— RICK BURGESS
*In loving memory of William
Bronner "Cornbread" Burgess.
Born in the arms of Jesus,
May 27, 2005–January 19, 2008*

If you just made a decision for Christ, please visit
http://www.sharingthefaith.com/followup.aspx
to assist you on your journey.